U0794219

航空服务类系列规划教材

国际航班客舱服务

International Flight Cabin Service

（活页式）

主编　沈　巧　　胡　蓓

西南交通大学出版社
·成　都·

图书在版编目（CIP）数据

国际航班客舱服务 = International Flight Cabin Service：汉英对照 / 沈巧，胡蓓主编. —成都：西南交通大学出版社，2023.1
ISBN 978-7-5643-9161-4

Ⅰ. ①国… Ⅱ. ①沈… ②胡… Ⅲ. ①民用航空－旅客运输－商业服务－高等学校－教材－汉、英 Ⅳ. ①F560.9

中国国家版本馆 CIP 数据核字（2023）第 008544 号

Guoji Hangban Kecang Fuwu

国际航班客舱服务

International Flight Cabin Service

主编 沈 巧 胡 蓓

责任编辑 孟 媛
封面设计 原谋书装

出版发行 西南交通大学出版社
（四川省成都市金牛区二环路北一段 111 号
西南交通大学创新大厦 21 楼）
邮政编码 610031
发行部电话 028-87600564 028-87600533
网址 http://www.xnjdcbs.com
印刷 四川玖艺呈现印刷有限公司

成品尺寸 185 mm × 260 mm
印张 9.5
字数 178 千
版次 2023 年 1 月第 1 版
印次 2023 年 1 月第 1 次
书号 ISBN 978-7-5643-9161-4
定价 28.00 元

课件咨询电话：028-81435775

PREFACE 前言

近年来，我国国际航线飞速发展，由中华人民共和国成立初期的几条航线发展到现在 1,600 多条。因此，培养能够快速适应国际航线乘务工作岗位的人才，培养有文化、有专业技能的空乘专业人才迫在眉睫。本书属空乘专业教材，根据乘务员国际航班客舱服务的工作需要，比较详细地介绍了国际航线的专业知识、国际航班的服务程序、各国 CIQ 知识、免税品销售服务等。

本书在编写过程中始终遵循“以学生为主体”的教学思想，理论知识以“必需”和“够用”为度，重点突出国际航班客舱服务的实践操作技能。在内容安排上以乘务工作的四个阶段为主线，以乘务员执行国际航班任务中的具体工作内容为重点，通过任务实施使学生迅速掌握工作要领。

本书为双语教材。部分章节内容通过中英文对照的形式帮助学生理解国际航班服务标准、服务程序，提高学生理解并使用英文进行国际航班客舱服务的能力。教材中的一部分国际航班服务标准来自国内外航空公司的乘务员工作手册，使用英文服务标准与中文要点介绍对照参考的形式使学生更易理解，并掌握其中的操作重点。

本书由沈巧、胡蓓主编。本书共分三个项目，分别为项目一国际航班规章及服务程序、项目二国际航线 CIQ 规章及单据填写、项目三机上免税品销售。其中，项目一包含七个单元，项目二包含两个单元，项目三包含两个单元。

在编写过程中，我们参考了大量的文献资料。在此，我们向参考过的文献的作者表示诚挚的谢意。由于编写时间仓促，编者水平有限，书中疏漏与不当之处在所难免，敬请广大读者批评指正。

编　者

CONTENTS

目　录

项目一　国际航班规章及服务程序

一、项目描述

据不完全统计，2011 年到 2018 年中国的国际航线旅客运输量年均增长率达到了17%左右，中国民航市场国际航线获得发展的同时，也面临着压力和挑战。

通过学习本项目，让同学们了解我国国际航线的发展情况，掌握我国主要航空集团和航空公司国际航线的运营情况和特点，掌握国际航空联盟的基本特征，了解国际知名航空公司的概况。并且，能使用标准英语完成飞行四个阶段的国际航班的经济舱服务程序，进行常见的酒类饮料服务。具备国际航线乘务员岗位要求的素养，有严谨的工作态度、较强的服务意识和良好的职业道德素养，将爱国、敬业、诚信、友善的精神融入国际航班旅客服务。

二、学习目标

（一）知识目标

1. 学生了解、掌握国际航班客舱乘务员岗位服务工作的基本要求、操作要点。
2. 学生掌握国际航线飞行各阶段的服务程序。
3. 学生掌握国际航线常见的酒类饮料知识及服务。

（二）能力目标

1. 学生能够按照服务标准完成国际航班客舱服务的基本操作程序，处理一般常见问题。
2. 能通过模拟国际航班情景训练，完成不同航程的国际航线经济舱的服务。

3. 学生能够使用英语完成客舱服务程序。

4. 学生能够按照要求完成常见的酒类饮料服务。

（三）素养目标

1. 具备国际航线乘务员岗位要求的素养，有严谨的工作态度、较强的服务意识和良好的职业道德素养。

2. 具有良好的职业道德与契约精神，良好的与人沟通的能力和团队合作精神。

3. 具有爱国、敬业、诚信、友善的精神，忠于职守，克己奉公，具有服务乘客，服务社会的职业精神。

单元一 国际航线概述

第一节 中国国际航线基本情况

一、中国国际航线发展迅速

2018 年上半年，中国民航国际航线旅客运输量共 3 112.5 万人次，同比增加 16.4%。同期国内航线旅客运输量共 2.66 亿人次，同比增加 11.9%。国际航线旅客运输量增速连续 5 个月超过国内航线。与此同时，国际航线给航司带来的收益增速也超过国内航线。

In the first half of 2018, China civil aviation carried 31.125 million passengers on international routes, up 16.4 percent year-on-year. During the same period, 266 million passengers were transported on domestic routes, up 11.9 percent year-on-year. The growth rate of passenger traffic on international routes has outpaced that on domestic routes for five consecutive months. At the same time, the revenue growth rate of international routes to airlines is also more than domestic routes.

从具体机场来看，增速最快的是规模较小、国际航线较少的小机场，甚至是支线机场，新开通国际航线让这些机场的国际旅客快速甚至成倍增长。国际航线新市场上升更快，主要原因是群众“钱包鼓了”，中南和西南地区国际航线旅客吞吐量增长最快。

In terms of specific airports, the fastest growth is seen in smaller airports with fewer international routes, and even in regional airports, where the number of international passengers increased rapidly or even doubled with the opening of new international routes. The new market of international airlines grew faster, mainly due to the people's "rich wallet". The passenger throughout of international routes in central and southern China and southwest China grew fastest.

较大型的省会机场、千万级机场国际旅客增长量也相当惊人。不少机场在航班时刻十分紧张、运力饱和的情况下仍然保持了高增长。武汉机场 2016 年增长接近 50%，南京、长沙、郑州、天津、重庆、成都机场也都有大幅增长。此外三大枢纽机场增长也很可观，其中广州机场增速超过 20%，首都机场也保持了两位数的增速。从往返地双向来看，2016 年增长最快的有两类，一类是从我国的大型枢纽机场到国外一般枢纽机场的航班，另一类是从我国一般枢纽机场到国外主要枢纽机场。这也表明新老市场各有不同的增长空间。

The growth of international passengers in larger provincial capital airports and ten-million-class airports is also quite astonishing. Many airports maintained high growth despite tight flight schedules and capacity saturation. Wuhan Airport grew by nearly 50% in 2016, while airports in Nanjing, Changsha, Zhengzhou, Tianjin, Chongqing and Chengdu also saw significant growth. In addition, the three major hub airports also saw impressive growth, with Guangzhou Airport growing by more than 20% and Beijing Capital Airport also maintaining double-digit growth.

In terms of round-trip, there are two types of flights with the fastest growth in 2016. One is the flight from China's large hub airports to foreign general hub airports, and the other is the flight from China's general hub airports to foreign major hub airports. It also suggests there is room for growth in both old and new markets.

我国的国际航线发展迅猛，专家认为主要原因是老百姓“钱包鼓了”。中国的黄金周都快成为世界的黄金周了，其间中国游客是世界各大旅游城市的主要客源。而且淡季也不淡，除了反季节出国游等因素之外，商务往来的旅客也越来越多。此外，我国航空公司实力日益强大是中国旅客走出去的重要支撑。国际化战略是很多航空公司近几年发展的重点。比如南方航空打造中国大陆至大洋洲、东南亚和南亚的第一门户，2016 年在广州地区的国际航线运力投入已超过国内航线。海南航空在 2016 年共开通国际航线 22 条，一年共新增 767 个往返航班，达到了历年开航之最。此外，一些国家签证条件的放松，自由行、免签地的增长也对我国旅客出境起到了促进作用。

International routes develop rapidly. China's golden week is on the verge of becoming the world's golden week, during which Chinese tourists are the main source of tourists in major tourist cities around the world. And the off-season is not weak, in addition to the seasonal overseas travel and other factors, business travelers are also becoming more and more.

In addition, the growing strength of China's airlines is an important support for Chinese travelers to go global. Internationalization strategy is the focus of many airlines' development in recent years. For example, China Southern Airlines has built the first gateway from the Chinese mainland to Oceania, Southeast Asia and South Asia. In 2016, the investment in the capacity of international routes in Guangzhou exceeded that of domestic routes. In 2016, Hainan Airlines opened a total of 22 international routes, adding 767 round-trip flights in a year, reaching the largest opening in the history. In addition, the relaxation of visa conditions in some countries and the growth of free travel and visa-free places have also promoted the outbound travel of Chinese tourists.

国际航线的快速发展也与地方政府的扶持息息相关。国际航线对地方经济有比较大的拉动作用，同时国际航线起步时又需要比较长的培育期，因此不少地方政府会给予国际航线补贴。“不沿海不靠边，对外开放靠蓝天”，通过民航发展将地方的产业优势放大延伸到国际市场，郑州机场就是一个典型案例，得到地方政府的大力支持，一跃成为重要的枢纽机场。国际民航组织有过一个统计，民航事业对地方经济的影响力是 1 比 8，目前来看，国际航线的价值又高于国内航线，这是一笔划算账。

The rapid development of international airlines is closely related to the support of local governments. International airlines have a relatively large driving effect on local economy, and at the same time, international airlines need a relatively long incubation period at the beginning, so many local governments will give subsidies to international airlines. "No coastal area, no edge, open to the outside depends on the blue sky". Through the development of civil aviation, the local industrial advantages are enlarged and extended to the international market. Zhengzhou Airport is a typical case, which has become an important hub airport with the strong support of the local government.

According to the International Civil Aviation Organization (ICAO), the impact of civil aviation on the local economy is 1 to 8. At present, the value of international flights is higher than that of domestic flights. This is a calculation.

二、中国国际航线竞争力需不断提升

国际航线将延续较好的增长势头，但是增速可能将放缓。2016 年，国际旅客的增速虽然高达 19.3%，但相比 2015 年超过 30%的增速来说，已经放缓，因为基数日益庞大。一些机场时刻资源紧张、运力增长有限，运送旅客数量不可能无限增长。此外，承运主体对于长航线的运力部署会更加谨慎，数字在增长，但是单位成本的收益压力也在增长。对航空公司来说，是“飞出去”后愈发激烈的国际竞争。加快国际化步伐以后，我国航空公司面临的是全球一流航空公司的竞争，国内、国际市场发展速度不同、竞争态势不同、标准规范不同，提升品牌知名度和竞争力是最迫切的任务。比如南方航空在重点发展的“袋鼠航线”这一市场上，早就有澳大利亚航空、新加坡航空、阿联酋航空等老牌知名航空企业在运营。

International airlines will continue to grow well, but the growth rate may slow down. In 2016, the growth rate of international passengers, though as high as 19.3 percent, has slowed from more than 30 percent in 2015, due to an increasingly large base. Some airports have limited resources and limited capacity growth, and the number of passengers can not grow indefinitely. In addition, carriers will be more cautious about deploying capacity on long routes. The number is increasing, but so is the revenue pressure on unit cost. For airlines, it is the increasingly fierce international competition after “flying out”.

After accelerating the pace of internationalization, Chinese airlines are faced with the competition from the world’s first-class airlines. Domestic and international markets have different development rates, different competition situations and different standards and norms. It is the most urgent task to improve brand awareness and competitiveness. For example, in the market of “Kangaroo route”, which China Southern focuses on developing, there are long been established well-known airlines such as Qantas Airlines, Singapore Airlines and Emirates Airlines in operation.

我国航空公司走到国际市场上，在经营经验和竞争力等方面还有较大的差距。首先表现在民航“逆差”还有点大。民航领域也可以跟国际贸易一样，引入逆差和顺差的概念。比如，以中美市场为例，中美往来大部分旅客是中国人，假设中国人比例为七成，如果国内航空公司运送的中国旅客少于七成，就可以算作“逆差”。逆差越大就说明出国搭乘自己本国航空公司的中国人越少，这个指标比单纯看增速更能说明我国民航业的竞争力。随着中国的市场越来越大，虎视眈眈的国际竞争者也越来越多。中国籍的国际旅客事实上被国外航空公司分流了很多，比如知名的阿联酋航空、新加坡航空、汉莎航空等，还有近些年新崛起的卡塔尔航空和土耳其航空，他们国内市场很有限，因此主要面向中国旅客提供航空服务。

When Chinese airlines go to the international market, there is still a big gap in business experience and competitiveness. First of all, in civil aviation "deficit" is still a little big. The concept of deficit and surplus can also be introduced into the civil aviation sector as in international trade. For example, take the Sino-US market as an example, the majority of passengers traveling between China and the US are Chinese. Assuming that 70% of the passengers are Chinese, if domestic airlines carry less than 70% of Chinese passengers, it can be considered as a "deficit". The bigger the deficit is, the fewer Chinese will go abroad to take their own airlines, which is a better indicator of the competitiveness of China's civil aviation industry than simply looking at the growth rate. As China's market grows bigger and bigger, more and more international competitors are eyeing it. In fact, Chinese international passengers are diverted a lot by foreign airlines, such as the well-known Emirates airlines, Singapore Airlines, Lufthansa airlines, etc., as well as the newly emerging Qatar Airways and Turkish Airlines in recent years, their domestic market is limited, so they mainly provide air services for Chinese passengers.

此外，差距还表现在“中转”这个指标上。中转主要体现的是“抢”国外旅客的能力，比争夺乘坐国际航班的本国旅客要更难。很多国际机场运送的旅客大部分都不是本国人，而是周边国家的旅客。而我国国际旅客增长主要还是中国旅客的贡献，吸引周边国家旅客的能力还比较欠缺。争取更多非中国籍的中转旅客，在眼下看来可能并不那么迫切，但是如果不从现在开始经营，国际旅客增长乏力的问题可能会慢慢显现出来。随着老龄化趋势的加剧，一二十年之后中国本土有钱有闲且有体力的出境游旅客会大量减少，国际航线的发展必然要依赖周边国家的旅客。

The gap is also reflected in the "transfer" index. Transits mainly reflect the ability to "compete" for foreign passengers, which is harder than competing for domestic passengers on international flights. Many international airports handle most passengers not from their own country, but from nearby countries. However, the growth of international tourists in China is mainly due to the contribution of Chinese tourists, and the ability to attract tourists from neighboring countries is still insufficient. Getting more non-Chinese transit passengers may not seem so urgent at the moment, but if we don't start now, the problem of weak international passenger growth could slowly become apparent. With the aggravation of the aging trend, in a decade or two, there will be a large decrease in the number of Chinese tourists with money, leisure and physical strength, and the development of international airlines will inevitably rely on passengers from neighboring countries.

三、中国国际航线发展提升路径

提升服务品质，缩小服务差距，是民航提升国际竞争力的重要因素。例如，从北京到新加坡，外航能给经济舱乘客提供 6 000 元和 2 000 元两种产品，我国不少航空公司却没有细分。服务不光要有基本功更要有加分项，尤其是国际航班有航程长等特点，我国在航班衔接、中转服务的便捷性上有很大的提升空间。此外，我国航空企业可以通过“互联网+”提升便捷性，提供全链条的运输服务。一张机票联通的不仅是两国，还联通了旅行社、大巴公司、专车、酒店、餐饮和景点门票，让乘客在购买机票的同时就能搞定一条龙的旅行服务。

Improving service quality and narrowing service gap are important factors for civil aviation to enhance international competitiveness. For example, from Beijing to Singapore, foreign airlines can provide economy passengers with 6,000 yuan and 2,000 yuan of two products, but many Chinese airlines do not have these choices.

The service should not only have basic skills, but also need to add items, especially international flights have long voyage and other characteristics, China has a lot of space to improve the convenience of flight connection and transfer services. In addition, Chinese aviation enterprises can improve the convenience and provide full-chain transport services through “Internet plus”. An air ticket not only connects the two countries, but also connects travel agencies, bus companies, private buses, hotels, restaurants and scenic spots tickets, allowing passengers to purchase tickets at the same time can get a one-stop travel service.

我国国际航线航空服务水平要上台阶，还应提高精细化程度。例如，从北京到新加坡的航班，新加坡航空给乘客提供两种经济舱选择。一种选择是往返需 6 000 元左右人民币，比头等舱便宜不少，但部分服务与头等舱一致，如提供拖鞋、红酒和丰富的餐食。另一种是该公司旗下的廉航产品，往返只要 2 000 元左右人民币，服务简化、没有免费餐食。针对经济舱旅客，我国很多航空公司可能就没有这样更进一步的细分，对旅客个性化需求的识别和满足能力不够。

China’s international aviation service level has to step up, but also to improve the degree of refinement. Singapore Airlines, for example, offers passengers two economy class options for flights from Beijing to Singapore. One option is a round trip of about RMB 6,000, much cheaper than first class, but with some of the same services, including slippers, wine and extensive meals. The other is the company's low-cost airline, which costs about RMB 2,000 for a round trip, with simplified service and no free meals. For economy class passengers, many airlines in China may not have such further segmentation, and lack the ability to identify and meet the personalized needs of passengers.

受益于国家“一带一路”政策，国际航线的发展迎来了前所未有的机遇。近几年，各大航空公司都在“一带一路”共建国家积极布局。民航局数据显示，国航在 2015 年连开 29 条国际航线，先后开通了北京至明斯克、布达佩斯、吉隆坡、孟买、科伦坡、伊斯兰堡等航线，并着力把成都建设成为面向欧洲、东南亚、南亚、中东和中亚的国际空中门户。2016 年，南航在“一带一路”上新增国际航线最多，新增广州—多伦多、深圳—雅加达等 10 多条国际航线。“一带一路”给民航带来的前景非常广阔，未来国际航线部署的行动方案与国家“一带一路”建设密切相关。但是，我国目前在这一沿线的布局还处在起步阶段，需要一个长期过程去运营。

我国民航国际航线的竞争力提升也有赖于我国在国际民航组织中话语权的提升。中国应更多地参与国际民航规章、标准的制定，通过加入联盟、代码共享、推广海外基地等方式促进旅客乘坐我国的国际航班，到达全球的各个角落。

Benefiting from China's The Belt and Road Initiative policy, the development of international airlines has ushered in unprecedented opportunities. In recent years, major airlines have been active in countries along the Belt and Road. According to the Civil Aviation Administration of China, Air China opened 29 international routes in 2015, including flights from Beijing to Minsk, Budapest, Kuala Lumpur, Mumbai, Colombo and Islamabad, and is striving to build Chengdu into an international air gateway to Europe, Southeast Asia, South Asia, the Middle East and Central Asia.

In 2016, China Southern Airlines added the most international routes along The Belt and Road, adding more than 10 international routes from Guangzhou to Toronto and Shenzhen to Jakarta. The Belt and Road Initiative brings a very broad prospect to civil aviation, and the action plan for the deployment of international airlines in the future is closely related to the construction of The Belt and Road Initiative in China. However, China's current layout along this line is still in the initial stage, need a long-term process to operate.

The competitiveness of China's civil aviation international routes also depends on the promotion of China's discourse power in the international Civil Aviation Organization.

China should participate more in the formulation of rules and standards of international civil aviation, and promote passengers to take international flights in China and reach all corners of the world by joining alliances, sharing codes and promoting overseas bases.

第二节　中国各主要航空公司国际航线发展简介

一、中国国际航空股份有限公司（AIR CHINA）

图 1-1-1　中国国际航空公司标志

中国国际航空股份有限公司简称“国航”，英文名称为“Air China Limited”，简称“Air China”，其前身中国国际航空公司成立于 1988 年。国航的企业标识由一只艺术化的凤凰和中国改革开放总设计师邓小平同志书写的“中国国际航空公司”以及英文“AIR CHINA”构成。国航标志颜色为中国传统的大红，造型以简洁舞动的线条展现凤凰姿态，同时又是英文“VIP”（尊贵客人）的艺术变形。国航推崇的凤凰精神的核心内涵是“传递吉祥，引领群伦，超越自我”。

Air China can trace its origins to 1988 when Air China International Corporation was established. The corporate logo of Air China depicts phoenix, a legendary bird worshiped by the nation since ancient times as a symbol of luck and happiness. With imagination stretched a bit, the way the logo is laid out recalls the English word “VIP”. The deep red color is used since it’s associated with anything happy and lucky in Chinese culture. The message conveyed by the whole design is that Air China commits itself to promoting the development of the country’s airline industry and offering pleasant travel experiences to passengers.

国航是中国唯一载国旗飞行的民用航空公司以及世界最大的航空联盟——星空联盟成员、2008 年北京奥运会航空客运合作伙伴，具有国内航空公司第一的品牌价值，在航空客运、货运及相关服务诸方面，均处于国内领先地位。国航于 2007 年 12 月加入星空联盟。作为星空联盟成员、中国唯一的载旗航空公司，国航运营着世界级的航空网络，每周为旅客提供超过 8 500 个航班，连接全球 40 个国家和地区的 184 个目的地。

Air China is China’s sole flag carrier and a member of the world’s largest airline alliance—Star Alliance. It was previously the official airline partner for the Beijing 2008

Olympic and Paralympic Games, and has been selected as an official partner for the Beijing 2022 Olympic and Paralympic Winter Games. Air China is China's largest airline by brand value (valued at RMB 197.236 billion by the World Brand Lab in Jun. 2021) and is a market leader in air passenger transportation, air cargo and other aviation services.

截至 2021 年 12 月 31 日，国航（含控股公司）共拥有以波音、空中客车为主的各型飞机 746 架，平均机龄 8.23 年；经营客运航线已达 672 条，通航国家及地区 25 个，通航城市 151 个，通过与星空联盟成员等航空公司的合作，将服务进一步拓展到 195 个国家（地区）的 1 300 个目的地。

As of December 31, 2021，Air China (including its holding company) owns a total of 746 aircrafts of various types, mainly by Boeing and Airbus, with an average lifespan of 8.23 years, operating 672 passenger routes to 151 cities in 25 countries and regions. Our service was further extended to 1,300 destinations in 195 countries(regions) through cooperation with airlines such as Star Alliance Members.

国航空中乘务队伍显示了国际化水准，日籍、韩籍、德籍乘务员陆续加盟，具有良好的职业素质和敬业精神，是旅客在蓝天上最好的朋友。他们持续推进让旅客“放心、顺心、舒心、动心”的“四心服务”工程，服务品质一直受到广大旅客的赞赏。

Air China is committed to providing passengers with "Four Cs" service: Credibility, Convenience, Comfort, and Choice. Its "PhoenixMiles" frequent flyer program has the longest history of any frequent flyer program in China. Air China has a strong domestic and international route network and sales network, and an extensive high quality customer base. It has become the preferred airline for many Chinese government agencies and corporate business customers.

从旅客航距看，国航的国际旅客行程最远。总周转量占比高，而旅客运输量占比低，说明国航的国际长航线旅客较多，因此旅客量相对较少。从国际旅客的人均航距来看，国航的国际旅客人均航距比其他两大航要长 1 000 千米左右，国航的国际长航线优势突显无疑。

In terms of passenger distance, Air China's international passengers travel the farthest. The proportion of total turnover is high, while the proportion of passenger transport is low, indicating that there are more passengers on the international long route of Air China, so the passenger volume is relatively small.

From the perspective of the per capita flight distance of international passengers, the per capita flight distance of international passengers of Air China is about 1,000 kilometers longer than that of the other two major airlines, and the advantage of Air China's international long routes is undoubtedly highlighted.

二、中国南方航空股份有限公司（CHINA SOUTHERN AIRLINES）

中国南方航空
CHINA SOUTHERN AIRLINES

图 1-1-2　中国南方航空公司标志

中国南方航空股份有限公司（以下简称南航），总部设在广州，以蓝色垂直尾翼镶红色木棉花为公司标志，是中国运输飞机最多、航线网络最发达、年客运量最大的航空公司。南航以建设“阳光南航”为使命，以“顾客至上、尊重人才、追求卓越、持续创新、爱心回报”为文化理念，以“成为顾客首选、员工喜爱的航空公司”为愿景，持续打造“中国最好、亚洲一流”的航空公司。

China Southern Airlines Company Limited, with world headquarters based in Guangzhou, has its company logo seen around the globe with a brilliant red kapok delicately adoring a blue vertical tail fin.

China Southern Airlines possesses the largest fleet and the most developed route network, and offers the largest passenger capacity among any airline in the People's Republic of China.

The airline radiates its distinctive cultural character of “Sunshine China Southern” and its mission continues to be “Connecting the World to Create a Better Life”.

南航年旅客运输量最高达到 1.52 亿人次，连续 43 年居中国各航空公司之首。南航年旅客运输量居亚洲第一、世界前列，货邮运输量世界前十（数据来源：国际航协）。截至 2021 年 12 月，南航运营包括波音 787、777、737 系列，空客 A330、A320 系列及商飞 ARJ21 等型号客货运输飞机超过 860 架。南航每天有 3 000 多个航班飞往全球 40 多个国家和地区、224 个目的地，航线网络 1 000 多条，提供座位数超过 50 万个。通过与美国航空、英国航空、卡塔尔航空、越南航空等合作伙伴密切合作，南航航线网络延伸到全球更多目的地。

China Southern Airlines has carried 152 million passengers a year, ranking first among Chinese airlines for 43 years in a row. The annual passenger transport volume of China Southern Airlines ranks first in Asia and top in the world, and the cargo transport volume ranks top ten in the world (data source: International Air Transport Association).

By December 2021, China Southern Airlines operates more than 860 passenger and cargo transport aircraft, including Boeing 787, 777 and 737 series, Airbus A330, A320 series and ARJ21.

China Southern Airlines operates more than 3,000 flights a day to 224 destinations in more than 40 countries and regions, with a network of more than 1,000 routes and offers more than 500,000 seats.

Working closely with partners such as American Airlines, British Airways, Qatar Airways and Vietnam Airlines, China Southern Airlines' route network extends to more destinations around the world.

近年来，南航全力打造广州—北京“双枢纽”，通过新开和优化航线网络，致力建设两大综合性国际航空枢纽。在广州，南航持续 10 年稳步建设“广州之路”(Canton Route)，服务“一带一路”和粤港澳大湾区。截至 2019 年年末，南航在广州白云机场的通航点达 163 个，其中国际及地区通航点 55 个。南航广州枢纽已成为中国大陆至大洋洲、东南亚的第一门户。广州与国内、东南亚主要城市形成“4 小时航空交通圈”，与全球主要城市形成“12 小时航空交通圈”。

In recent years, China Southern Airlines has made every effort to build a “dual hub” between Guangzhou and Beijing, and is committed to building two comprehensive international aviation hubs by opening and optimizing the route network. In Guangzhou, China Southern Airlines has been steadily building the “Canton Route” for 10 years to serve the “One Belt, One Road” and the Guangdong-Hong Kong-Macao Greater Bay Area.

By the end of 2019, China Southern Airlines had 163 routes in Guangzhou Baiyun Airport, including 55 international and regional routes. Guangzhou Hub of China Southern Airlines has become the first gateway from Chinese mainland to Oceania and Southeast Asia. Guangzhou has formed a “4-hour air traffic circle” with major cities in China and Southeast Asia, and a “12-hour air traffic circle” with major cities around the world.

三、中国东方航空股份有限公司（CHINA EASTERN AIRLINES）

图 1-1-3　中国东方航空公司标志

中国东方航空股份有限公司（以下简称东航）总部位于上海，作为中国三大国有航空公司之一，前身可追溯到 1957 年 1 月原民航上海管理处成立的第一支飞行中队。在经历一系列发展沿革后，1988 年正式成立中国东方航空公司，1997 年分别在纽约、香港、上海证券交易所成功挂牌上市，是中国民航首家三地上市的航空公司。

Headquartered in Shanghai, China Eastern Airlines Corporation Limited (CEA) is among China's three major airlines. It originated from the first squadron established by former Civil Aviation Administration of Shanghai in January, 1957. After a series of reform, CEA was founded in 1988 and listed on New York, Hong Kong and Shanghai stock markets in 1997, becoming the first airline listed on three markets together.

作为天合联盟成员，东航的航线网络通达全球 170 个国家和地区的 1 036 个目的地，每年为全球超过 1.3 亿旅客提供服务，旅客运输量位列全球前十。“东方万里行”常旅客可享受联盟 19 家航空公司的会员权益及全球超过 790 间机场贵宾室。

As a member of SkyTeam Alliance, CEA has extended its flight network to 1,036 destinations in 170 countries and regions via close cooperation with SkyTeam Alliance member airlines. The annual passenger turnover of CEA exceeds more than 130 million, ranking top 10 among global airlines. Eastern Miles members can enjoy the membership rights of SkyTeam's 19 member airlines and more than 790 airport VIP lounges worldwide.

东航的机队规模达 760 余架（2022 年），是全球规模航企中最年轻的机队之一，拥有中国规模最大、商业和技术模式领先的互联网宽体机队。

CEA operates a modern fleet of over 760 aircrafts（2022）, which is one of the youngest fleets in major airlines worldwide. Moreover, it boasts the largest-scale in-flight Wi-Fi wide-bodied fleet with leading commercial and technical models in China.

东航在国内拥有京沪“两市四场”双核心枢纽和西安、昆明等区域枢纽，业务范围实现省会城市及千万级以上机场的全覆盖，并在全球设有 108 个海内外分支机构。公司近年来开通多条“一带一路”国际新航线，积极构建连通全球的“空中丝绸之路”。

China Eastern owns two domestic core hubs in Beijing and Shanghai with four airports, and regional hubs in Xi'an, Kunming and other cities. The scope of business in China covers all airports at municipalities and provincial capitals as well as those with above 10-million-passenger turnover. At present, CEA operates 108 domestic and overseas branches across the globe. In recent years, CEA has successively launched new routes along the Belt and Road, plays a positive role in building a Silk Road in the air.

四、四川航空股份有限公司（SICHUAN AIRLINES）

图 1-1-4　四川航空股份有限公司标志

熊猫之路，连接世界。四川航空股份有限公司（以下简称川航）总部位于成都。作为中国最具特色的航空公司之一，川航以安全为品牌核心价值，持续安全飞行 34 年（2022 年），现运营中国国内最大的全空客机队超过 170 架飞机，执飞国内外航线 460 余条，为全球旅客提供深具“中国元素 四川味道”的航空服务，品牌价值超过六百亿，并成为第 31 届世界大学生夏季运动会官方合作伙伴。

Sichuan Airlines Co., LTD. (hereinafter referred to as Sichuan Airlines) is headquartered in Chengdu. As one of the most distinctive airlines in China, Sichuan Airlines takes safety as its core brand value and has been flying safely for 34 years (2022). Now, Sichuan Airlines operates the largest Airbus fleet in China with more than 170 aircrafts, flies more than 460 domestic and foreign routes, and provides passengers around the world with a deep “Sichuan flavor of Chinese elements” air service, with a brand value of more than 60 billion yuan. And it became the official partner of the 31st Summer Universiade.

随着成都迈入双机场时代，川航正式开启“两场一体”运行新时代。川航按照中国民航规划和四川省委省政府战略部署，构筑高效的航班波结构，打造以成都为核心，辐射欧洲、大洋洲、北美洲、非洲以及东南亚、东北亚的中转网络；依托全空客货机机队，进一步整合航空物流地面综合服务，为客户提供定制化、多样化和专业化高端物流解决方案。通过“熊猫之路”客货齐飞，川航正实现多元化、高质量发展，为国家、地方经济建设贡献力量。

As Chengdu enters the era of double airports, Sichuan Airlines officially opens a new era of “two airports in one” operation. According to the civil aviation planning of China and the strategic deployment of Sichuan Provincial Government, Sichuan Airlines has built an efficient flight wave structure, and built a transit network with Chengdu as the core, radiating to Europe, Oceania, North America, Africa, Southeast Asia and Northeast Asia.

Relying on the passenger and cargo aircraft fleets, the company will further integrate integrated ground services of aviation logistics and provide customers with customized, diversified and professional high-end logistics solutions. Through the "Panda Road", Sichuan Airlines is realizing diversified and high-quality development, contributing to the national and local economic construction.

五、厦门航空（XIAMEN AIRLINES）

图 1-1-5　厦门航空公司标志

厦门航空成立于 1984 年，总部位于中国东南沿海的福建省厦门市，是中国首家按现代企业制度运行的航空公司。经过多年的持续发展，厦航现已成为中国民航保持盈利最长的航空公司，也是自 1987 年以来，全球唯一实现连续 35 年盈利的大中型客运航空公司。截至 2021 年 12 月，厦航机队规模达到 209 架飞机，目前运营国内外航线 400 余条，年旅客运输量近 4 000 万人次，已有超过 1 600 万人加入厦航常旅客计划。在国际航协 270 多家成员航空公司中，厦航的收入规模排名列前 30 位，旅客运输量跻身前 15 位，盈利能力更是进入前 10 位。

Headquartered in Xiamen City, Fujian Province–the southeast coast of China, Xiamen Airlines is founded in 1984 as China's first airlines created in accordance with the modern corporate system. After years of continuous development, Xiamen Airlines has become the most profitable airlines in China's civil aviation industry, and the only large and medium-sized passenger airline in the world that has made profits for 35 consecutive years since 1987. As of December 2021, Xiamen Airlines has a fleet of 209 aircrafts, and currently operates more than 400 domestic and international routes, carrying nearly 40 million passengers annually. More than 16 million people have joined Xiamen Airlines' frequent flyer program. Among the more than 270 member airlines of IATA, Xiamen Airlines ranks top 30 in terms of revenue, top 15 in terms of passenger transport volume and top 10 in terms of profitability.

厦航是天合联盟成员，航空承运人代码为“MF”，航线网络覆盖全中国、辐射东南亚和东北亚，随着阿姆斯特丹、悉尼、纽约、洛杉矶等洲际航线的陆续开通，实现了航线网络对欧洲、美洲和大洋洲的全覆盖，并借助天合联盟将航线网络延伸至全球。

Xiamen Airlines, a member of the SkyTeam Alliance with an air carrier code of "MF", forms a network covering the entire China and with a strong presence in Southeast and Northeast Asia. In recent years, as new intercontinental routes to Amsterdam, Sydney, New York, Los Angeles, etc. were opened consecutively, its network has prospered and reached Europe, America and Oceania, and extended to all major destinations around the world via SkyTeam Alliance.

多年来，厦航在保证航空安全、提升服务品质方面做出了不懈努力，累计安全飞行达到 700 万小时，获评民航局颁发的“飞行安全五星奖”，连续七年被中国旅客评为“最佳航空公司”。2016 年 3 月，厦航荣获第二届中国质量奖，成为中国服务业首家获此殊荣的企业，同时也是中国民航唯一获奖的航空公司。2020 年 12 月，世界著名航空服务测评机构 APEX 授予厦航 “五星级国际航空公司”。

Over the years, Xiamen Airlines has made unremitting efforts to ensure aviation safety and improve service quality. It has flown 7 million hours safely and been awarded the “Five-star Flight Safety Award” by the Civil Aviation Administration. Xiamen Airlines has been awarded the “Best Airlines” by Chinese passengers for seven consecutive years. In March 2016, Xiamen Airlines won the second China Quality Award, becoming the first company in China’s service industry to receive this award, and the only airline in CAAC to receive this award. In December 2020, Xiamen Airlines was awarded “Five-star International Airlines” by APEX, a world-renowned aviation service evaluation organization.

六、海南航空(HAINAN AIRLINES)

海南航空
HAINAN AIRLINES

图 1-1-6　海南航空公司标志

海南航空控股股份有限公司于 1993 年 1 月成立，起步于中国最大的经济特区和自由贸易港——海南省，是中国发展最快和最有活力的航空公司之一，致力于为旅客提供全方位无缝隙的航空服务，打造安全舒适的旅行体验。

Hainan Airlines was established in January, 1993 in Hainan Province, China’s largest special economic zone and free trade port. As one of the fastest growing airlines in China, Hainan Airlines is committed to providing passengers with comprehensive, seamless and high-quality service experience.

1993 年至今，海南航空连续安全运行 29 年。2021 年海南航空及旗下控股子公司共运营国内外航线近 1 800 条，其中国内航线近 1 700 条，涉及内陆所有省、自治区、直辖市，国际航线近 100 条，包括定期客运、复工复学包机和客改货等航班，航线覆盖亚洲、欧洲、非洲、北美洲和大洋洲，通航境外 30 个城市。海南航空积极响应国家倡议，融入“一带一路”建设，专注打造国际国内高效互动的、品质型、规模化的卓越型世界级航空网络。积极落实“民航强国”发展战略，在北京、广州、海口、深圳等 24 个城市建立航空营运基地/分公司。

Since 1993, Hainan Airlines has been operating safely for 29 consecutive years. As of 2021, Hainan Airlines and its holding subsidiaries operate nearly 1,800 domestic and international routes. There are nearly 1,700 domestic routes, involving all inland provinces, autonomous regions and municipalities directly under the Central Government. There are nearly 100 international routes, including scheduled passenger flights, charter flights for resumption of work and school, and passenger-to-cargo flights, covering Asia, Europe, Africa, North America and Oceania, and navigating to 30 overseas cities. Actively responding to The Belt and Road Initiative, Hainan Airlines has focused on building a world-class airline network with efficient interaction, quality and scale at home and abroad. To implement the Strategy of Civil Aviation Powerful Country, Hainan Airlines and its holding subsidiaries have established aviation operation bases/branches in 24 cities including Beijing, Guangzhou, Haikou and Shenzhen.

海南航空作为中国内地唯一一家 SKYTRAX 五星航空公司，凭借优质的服务水平蝉联 SKYTRAX“中国最佳员工服务”奖，并荣获“中国最佳客舱乘务员”奖，在“全球最佳客舱乘务员”奖项中世界排名第七名等多个奖项。

Hainan Airlines, as the only SKYTRAX 5-Star airlines in the mainland of China, has won the SKYTRAX “Best Airline Staff in China” award for its high-quality service, won the “Best Cabin Crew in China” award, ranked seventh in the world in the “The World’s Best Airline Cabin Crew” award, and other awards.

第三节　世界航空联盟

航空公司联盟组织是建立在双边合作的基础上，多家航空公司间的一种多边管理模式，其目的是提升网络、产品和服务规模优势，为旅客提供更方便和优质的服务，提升市场份额和航空公司收益水平。

Airline alliance is a multilateral management mode between several airlines based on bilateral cooperation. Its purpose is to improve the scale advantage of network, products and services, provide passengers with more convenient and high-quality services, and improve market share and airline earnings.

随着经济全球化的深入，航空公司联盟化已成为世界民航业趋势。有效利用联盟的强劲枢纽做辐射，通过代码共享、常旅客计划共享手段，联盟成员在不需要投入任何资源的情况下就能增加运力和航班密度。如果联盟伙伴的航线网络是互补的，则可有效提升客座率，增加旅客运输量，并伴随一定程度的成本下降。目前世界上主流的航空联盟共三家，分别是：Star Alliance（星空联盟）、One World（寰宇一家）和 SkyTeam（天合联盟）。

With the deepening of economic globalization, airline alliance has become the trend of the world civil aviation industry. By effectively leveraging the alliance's strong hubs, through code-sharing and frequent-flier program sharing, alliance members can increase capacity and flight density without committing any resources. It can effectively improve the passenger load factor, increase the passenger traffic, and reduce the cost.

At present, there are three mainstream airline alliances in the world, including Star Alliance, One World and SkyTeam.

一、航空联盟建立的原因

代码共享：航空联盟可提供更大的航空网络。很多航空联盟的开始都是来自几个航空公司之间的代码共享网络发展而成。

资源共用：共用维修设施、运作设备、职员，相互支援地勤与空厨作业以减低成本。

降低成本：由于成本减少，乘客可以用更低廉的价格购买机票。

调配灵活：航班开出时间更灵活有弹性。

减少转机：转机次数减少，乘客可更方便地抵达目的地。

积分互通：乘客在旅游奖励计划如亚洲万里通使用同一账户乘搭不同航空公司均可赚取飞行里数。

Code sharing: Airline alliances can provide larger airline networks. Many airline alliances began as codeshare networks between several airlines.

Sharing of resources: Sharing of maintenance facilities, operation equipment and staff, with mutual support of ground handling and operations to reduce costs.

Lower costs: Passengers can buy tickets at lower prices because of reduced costs.

Flexible deployment: Flight departure time is more flexible.

Fewer transfers: Passengers can get to their destination more easily with fewer transfers.

Bonus points: Passengers can earn miles flying on different airlines using the same account in travel incentive schemes such as Asia Miles.

二、全球三大航空联盟

1. Star Alliance（星空联盟）

图 1-1-7 星空联盟标志

星空联盟（Star Alliance）成立于 1997 年，是第一个全球航空联盟，其名字和标志上星形图案的五个部分代表着五大创始航空公司：北欧航空、泰国国际航空、加拿大航空、汉莎航空和美国联合航空。星空联盟是目前世界上最大的航空联盟，总部在德国法兰克福。到目前为止，星空联盟拥有 26 家正式成员（2022 年），星空联盟的优势在于成员数量多。新航、全日空、汉莎，包括新西兰已经是星空联盟的标杆航空公司。国内的航空公司里，国航和深航属于星空联盟。

Star Alliance was founded in 1997 as the first global airline alliance, with the five parts of the star on its name and logo representing the five founding airlines: SAS, Thai Airways International, Air Canada, Lufthansa, and United Airlines. Star Alliance is currently the world's largest airline alliance, headquartered in Frankfurt, Germany. So far, Star Alliance has 26 full members（2022）, the Star Alliance advantage is the number of members.

Singapore Airlines, All Nippon Airways and Lufthansa, including New Zealand, are already Star Alliance's benchmark carriers.

Among Chinese airlines, Air China and Shenzhen Airlines belong to the Star Alliance.

星空联盟成员航空公司包括许多世界顶级的航空公司，以及规模较小、更具区域性的航空公司。它们共同提供了与世界上几乎所有目的地的便捷连接。每家航空公司都保持着自己的个人风格和文化特征，为联盟带来了丰富的多样性和多元文化。同时，每家航空公司都有一个共同的承诺，那就是提供最高标准的安全和客户服务。

Star Alliance's member airlines include many of the world's top aviation companies as well as smaller, more regional carriers. Together, they offer easy connections to almost any destination in the world. Each airline maintains its own individual style and cultural identity, bringing the richness of diversity and multiculturalism to the Alliance. At the same time each airline shares a common dedication to the highest standards of safety and customer service.

图 1-1-8　星空联盟成员航空公司

2. SkyTeam（天合联盟）

图 1-1-9　天合联盟标志

天合联盟（SkyTeam）于 2000 年由法国航空、达美航空、墨西哥国际航空和大韩航空联合成立，2004 年荷兰皇家航空亦成为其会员，成为全球第二大航空联盟。今日的天合联盟成员数已发展到五大洲 18 个之多（2022 年），是迄今为止最年轻、规模第二的航空联盟。天合联盟依然在积极招募新会员中。

The SkyTeam alliance was formed in 2000 by Air France, Delta Air Lines, Aeromexico and Korean Air Lines. In 2004, KLM joined SkyTeam, making it the world's second largest airline alliance. Today, SkyTeam has grown to 18 members on five continents（2022）, making it the youngest and second largest aviation alliance to date. SkyTeam is still actively recruiting new members.

图 1-1-10　天合联盟成员航空公司

3. One World（寰宇一家）

图 1-1-11　寰宇一家标志

寰宇一家（One World）是全球第三大的航空联盟，于 1999 年成立，初时总部位于加拿大温哥华，其后于 2011 年正式宣布把总部迁往美国纽约市。其成员航空公司及其附属航空公司在航班时间、票务、代码共享、乘客转机、飞行常客计划、机场贵宾室及降低支出等多方面进行合作。寰宇一家成员航空公司包括：柏林航空、美国航空、英国航空、马来西亚航空、澳洲航空、芬兰航空、日本航空、国泰航空、西班牙国家航空、智利国家航空、卡塔尔航空、皇家约旦航空等。

One World is the world's third largest airline alliance. Founded in 1999, it was originally headquartered in Vancouver, Canada. In 2011, it officially announced that it would move its headquarters to New York City, USA. Its member airlines and their affiliates cooperate on flight schedules, ticketing, code sharing, passenger transfers, frequent flyer programs, airport lounges and cost reduction. One World member airlines include: Berlin Airlines American Airlines, British Airways, Malaysia Airlines, Qantas Airways, Finnair, Japan Airlines, Cathay Pacific, Qatar Airways, etc.

图 1-1-12　寰宇一家联盟航空公司

第四节　新加坡航空国际航班服务介绍

一、新加坡航空有限公司简介(Singapore Airlines)

图 1-1-13　新加坡航空公司标志

新加坡航空公司是 SkyTrax 五星级航空公司、星空联盟成员，其客运航线网络覆盖 35 个国家的 65 个目的地。新加坡航空自成立以来，赢得了创新市场领先者的荣誉，同时可提供优质服务和高质量产品。新加坡航空品牌在航空界中已广为人知，尤其是在安全、服务质量和革新风格方面。新加坡航空公司一直被誉为最舒适和最安全的航空公司之一。

Singapore Airlines is a SkyTrax five-star airline, a member of the Star Alliance, with a passenger route network covering 65 destinations in 35 countries. Since its inception, Singapore Airlines has earned the reputation of being an innovative market leader while providing quality service and high quality products.

Singapore Airlines is well known in the world, especially for safety, quality of service and innovative style. Singapore Airlines has a reputation as one of the most comfortable and safest airlines.

二、新航头等舱、商务舱服务特色

1. 豪华套房（Suites）

新加坡航空公司豪华套房独家配置于 A380 客机，为新航贵宾提供专属的静谧空间。每间套房都配有活动拉门和窗帘，套房以细致皮革和精美花梨木内饰，色调温馨。

Exclusive to the A380, Singapore Airlines Deluxe Suite offers exclusive quiet space for Singapore Airlines guests. Each suite is fitted with sliding doors and curtains, and the suites are furnished in delicate leather and exquisite rosewood interiors in warm hues.

2. 头等舱（First Class）

新加坡航空公司顶级设计的全新头等舱，安置八个尊荣独享的座位，配置于新航全新的波音 777-300ER 客机以及特定的波音 777-300 客机。其他机型的头等舱座椅间距为 60 英寸（运营于部分波音 777-200 机型），间距为 64 英寸头等舱座椅（运营于部分波音 777-300 机型），乘客将拥有自己的 10.4 英寸液晶显示屏和防噪声耳机，以及音频和视频的娱乐点播服务（AVOD），同时还有大量电影及流行电视节目随时随地供选择。

Singapore Airlines'new first-class cabin is designed to accommodate eight exclusive seats on Singapore Airlines'new Boeing 777-300ER and selected Boeing 777-300 aircraft.

Passengers will have their own 10.4-inch LCD screens and noise-blocking headphones on other models with seats 60 inches apart (on some 777-200 models) and 64 inches apart (on some 777-300 models), and audio and video entertainment on Demand (AVOD), as well as a wide selection of movies and popular TV shows anytime, anywhere.

3. 商务舱（Business Class）

新加坡航空公司全新的商务舱目前是世界上有史以来最宽敞的商务客舱，配备有同类最大的座椅和全平躺椅。全新中程商务舱里，乘客可以在全新的中程倾斜平躺式座椅上伸展身体，惬意休息。每个座椅都采用了精美的优质皮革材质。另有可调节的座椅预设模式、靠枕和腰靠。

Singapore airlines' new business class is currently the most spacious business class, equipped with the whole flat deck chair. New intermediate business class has lie-flat seats stretch. Each seat is adopted the fine quality leather material, the adjustable seat mode, the default mode pillows.

三、新航经济舱

新航最新经济舱座位配置于波音 777-300ER、A380 和 A330-300 飞机。乘客可依偎于温暖的纪梵希绒毯中，用专属的 LCD 显示屏惬意地观赏至爱节目。除了这些特色之外，还可以品尝由新航著名的国际烹饪顾问团队精心烹制的美味佳肴，配以无与伦比的精选美酒，享受备受同行赞誉的机上服务。

Singapore Airlines' latest economy class seats are available on Boeing 777-300ER, A380 and A330-300 aircraft. Passengers can snuggle up in warm Givenchy blankets and watch their favorite shows on their own LCD screens.

In addition to these features, passengers can enjoy delicious dishes prepared by Singapore Airlines' renowned international Culinary Advisory team, paired with an unparalleled selection of fine wines, and enjoy peer acclaimed in-flight service.

图 1-1-14　新加坡航空经济舱中式餐食

思考与练习

Practice

一、简答题 Short Answer Questions

1. 国际航线与国内航线有什么区别？请从飞行航线、服务程序、机组要求等方面简述。What's the difference between international and domestic flights? Please briefly describe flight routes, service procedures, crew requirements, etc.

2. 中国境内有哪些航空公司加入星空联盟？

Which airlines in China have joined Star Alliance?

3. 寰宇一家航空联盟在全球有哪些业务合作？举例说明。

What are the global business partnerships of the One World alliance? Give an example.

二、多选题 Multiple Choice Questions

1. 关于国际航班特点说法正确的是：

A. 夜间飞行应该确保旅客得到良好的休息，尽力营造良好的休息环境。

B. 随时关注旅客需求，及时提供相应服务。

C. 增强客舱巡视，随时关注客舱安全。

D. 在提供二餐的航线中，乘务长可根据乘客休息情况自行调整第二餐用餐时间。

What is true about the characteristics of international flights?

A. Night flight should ensure that passengers get a good rest and try to create a good rest environment.

B. Pay attention to the needs of passengers at any time and provide corresponding services in time.

C. Enhance cabin patrol and pay attention to cabin safety at all times.

D. In airlines that provide second meal, the purser can adjust the time of second meal according to the rest of passengers.

2. The world's three largest airline alliances are:

A. Star Alliance.

B. One World.

C. SkyTeam.

D. skytrax.

3.下列关于国际航班特点说法正确的有：

A. 夜航较多。

B. 乘务员工作时间长，轮班休息。

C. 可能会发多次餐食。

D. 飞行时间有长也有短。

Which of the following statements about the characteristics of international flights are true?

A. More night flights.

B. Flight attendants work long hours and take shifts to rest.

C. Multiple meals may be served.

D. There are long and short flights.

单元二　国际航班客舱服务规章

第一节　国际航班服务概述

一、客舱乘务员安全职责

客舱乘务员是机组必需成员，是保障飞行运行安全的人员之一，其主要职责是保证客舱安全。

在滑行、起飞前、着陆过程中或空中“系好安全带”信号灯亮时以及机长要求的任何时候，乘务员除完成保障飞机和机上人员安全的任务外其他时间应当坐在值勤位置并系好安全带和肩带。

根据民航局颁发的 96 号文件《关于加强客舱安全管理工作的意见》，航空公司设立的服务标准应充分考虑客舱乘务员完成的时间，以确保起飞后 20 分钟或平飞至落地前 30 分钟能完成所有旅客服务程序。飞机进入下降阶段后不应再为旅客提供餐食服务。飞行过程中，乘务长有权根据实际情况调整服务程序，保障 30 分钟前完成客舱服务工作，保障乘务员有足够的精力履行客舱安全职责。

国际线普通舱乘务员需经过国际运输、外事知识、国际航线、CIQ、应急生存、应急撤离、急救、供餐服务等训练，经考试合格后才可取得国际线普通舱乘务员资格。

二、客舱乘务员服务职责（以空客 A320 机型 6 人制为例）

1. 带班乘务长（PS1）

带班乘务长职责详见表 1-2-1。

表 1-2-1　带班乘务长职责

Duty	Overview of the Responsibilities
Purser（PS1）	➢ Supervise and manage cabin safety and service throughout the whole process. ➢ Be responsible for the inspection of service equipment and emergency equipment. ➢ Check CIQ declaration documents. ➢ Responsible for handling emergency situations during the flight.

（1）全程监督管理客舱安全和服务。

（2）负责本号位的服务设备及紧急设备检查工作。根据航班特点部署服务工作。

（3）签收各种文件，与相关单位业务协调。

（4）国际航线检查 CIQ 申报单据，并办理相关手续。

（5）负责发放《旅客意见卡》，征求旅客对航班服务工作的意见。负责航班中特色服务方案的实施。

（6）负责处理航班中各种特殊情况。

（7）起飞前，了解旅客人数和特殊旅客的情况，并向其他乘务员传达。负责 VIP 服务。

（8）负责下达操作滑梯的指令，并操作 L1 舱门的滑梯手柄与 FS2 确认。通过内话听取各号位乘务员对舱门操作情况的报告。

（9）旅客登机时，负责在 L1 舱门处迎客，并数客。

（10）负责机上娱乐系统的播放。

（11）航班任务完成后，负责组织讲评，认真填写《乘务长工作单》。

（12）紧急情况下，按机长的指令，指挥乘务员应急处置，及时疏散旅客。

2. 2 号位乘务员（FS2）

2 号位乘务员职责详见表 1-2-2。

表 1-2-2　2 号乘务员职责

Duty	Overview of the Responsibilities
First Class Flight Attendant（FS2）	➢ In charge of first class cabin service. ➢ Be responsible for the inspection of service equipment and emergency equipment. ➢ Responsible for safety inspection of first class cabin. ➢ Responsible for broadcasting.

（1）负责头等舱厨房、客舱服务工作，以及为机组服务。

（2）负责清点、检查头等舱餐食和服务供应品以及特色航班所需物品，并负责做好头等舱的各项准备。

（3）负责责任区域的服务设备及紧急设备检查工作。

（4）旅客登机时，负责安排头等舱旅客就座，头等舱无旅客时，协助 SS3 疏导旅客。

（5）负责监控头等舱卫生间的清理。

（6）起飞、下降前，负责头等舱客舱、厨房、卫生间安全检查工作。负责操作 R1 舱门滑梯手柄，与 PS 互相确认完成情况。

（7）负责广播服务。

（8）在头等舱无旅客的情况下，负责协助 Y 舱工作。在乘务长的安排下落实特色服务方案的实施。紧急情况下，听从指挥，按照要求组织旅客脱离。

3. 3 号位乘务员（SS3）

3 号位乘务员职责详见表 1-2-3。

表 1-2-3　3 号位乘务员职责

Duty	Overview of the Responsibilities
Economy Class Flight Attendant（SS3）	➢ Responsible for passenger service in row 3—8. ➢ Responsible for the safety inspection of passengers in rows 3—8. ➢ In case of emergency, follow instructions and organize passengers to evacuate.

（1）负责客舱工作，负责整理书报、杂志。

（2）负责经济舱 3—8 排区域内的旅客服务。

（3）负责责任区域的服务、客舱设备及紧急设备检查工作。旅客登机时，负责引导 3—8 排旅客入座。

（4）起飞、下降前，负责经济舱 3—8 排旅客安全检查工作。在乘务长的安排下落实特色服务方案的实施。紧急情况下，听从指挥，按照要求组织旅客脱离。

4. 4 号位乘务员（SS4）

4 号位乘务员职责详见表 1-2-4。

表 1-2-4　4 号位乘务员职责

Duty	Overview of the Responsibilities
Economy Class Flight Attendant（SS4）	➢ Responsible for passenger service in row 9—16. ➢ Responsible for the safety inspection of passengers in rows 9—16 and toilets in the rear cabin. ➢ In case of emergency, follow instructions and organize passengers to evacuate. ➢ Responsible for emergency exit confirmation.

（1）负责客舱工作，负责整理书报、杂志。

（2）负责经济舱 9—16 排区域内的旅客服务。

（3）负责责任区域的服务、客舱设备及紧急设备检查工作。负责清理卫生间及分放卫生用品。

（4）旅客登机时，负责引导经济舱 9—16 排的旅客入座。

（5）起飞、下降前，负责经济舱 9—16 排旅客及后舱卫生间的安全检查工作。负责应急出口的确认并在关舱门前向乘务长汇报，做到全程监控。在乘务长的安排下落实特色服务方案的实施。

（6）紧急情况下，听从指挥，按照要求组织旅客脱离。

5. 5 号位乘务员（SS5）

5 号位乘务员职责详见表 1-2-5。

表 1-2-5　5 号位乘务员职责

Duty	Overview of the Responsibilities
Economy Class Flight Attendant（SS5）	➢ Responsible for passenger service in row 17—28. ➢ Responsible for the safety inspection of passengers in rows 17—28 and toilets in the rear cabin. ➢ In case of emergency, follow instructions and organize passengers to evacuate. ➢ Responsible for operating L2 door slide handle and check.

（1）负责客舱工作，负责整理书报、杂志，国际航线 CIQ 申报单据的准备。

（2）负责责任区域的服务、客舱设备及紧急设备检查工作。负责清理卫生间及分放卫生用品。

（3）负责协助 SS6 的厨房工作。

（4）旅客登机时，负责引导经济舱 17—28 排的旅客入座。

（5）起飞、下降前，负责经济舱 17—28 排旅客及后卫生间的安全检查工作。负责操作 L2 舱门滑梯手柄，与 SS6 互相确认。

（6）在乘务长的安排下落实特色服务方案的实施。

（7）紧急情况下，听从指挥，按照要求组织旅客脱离。

6. 6 号位乘务员（SS6）

6 号位乘务员职责详见表 1-2-6。

表 1-2-6　6 号位乘务员职责

Duty	Overview of the Responsibilities
Economy Class Flight Attendant（SS6）	➢ Responsible for the galley work. ➢ Responsible for the preparation of economy class catering. ➢ In case of emergency, follow instructions and organize passengers to evacuate. ➢ Responsible for operating R2 door slide handle and check.

（1）负责普通舱后厨房工作及客舱供应、补位工作。

（2）负责责任区域的服务设备及紧急设备检查工作。

（3）负责清点、检查、签收餐食及服务供应品，并向乘务长报告配餐情况。负责经济舱餐饮车准备工作。

（4）负责检查后厨房设备及餐饮车等。

（5）旅客登机时，负责在后厨房疏导最后几排的旅客入座。在 L2 舱门有客梯的情况下，负责数客，并报告乘务长。起飞、下降前，负责后厨房安全检查工作。

（6）负责操作 R2 舱门滑梯手柄，与 SS5 互相确认完成情况后向乘务长报告。在乘务长的安排下落实特色服务方案的实施。

（7）紧急情况下，听从指挥，按照要求组织旅客脱离。

三、空客各机型乘务员配备标准

1. 最低编制

一般情况下，根据民航局规定，在进行飞行运行时，每架载运旅客的飞机上，至少安排表 1-2-7 所示人数的乘务员。

表 1-2-7　不同机型乘务员最低人数要求

Aircraft Type	Cabin Crew
A-319	4名
A-320	4名
A-321	5名
A-330	8名

2. 满员编制

为满足航线运行要求，应按照民航局规章在最低编制的基础上增加乘务员人数。但最多不超过表 1-2-8 所示人数限制。

表 1-2-8　不同机型乘务员最高人数要求

Aircraft Type	Cabin Crew
A-319	5名
A-320	6名
A-321	7名
A-330	12名

注意：无论何种编制，每架载运旅客的飞机上均包含一名主任乘务长/乘务长，且 A330 机型至少还应含一名区域乘务长。

四、国际航班经济舱服务程序简介

国际航班经济舱服务程序详见表 1-2-9。

表 1-2-9　国际航班经济舱服务程序

Phase of Flight	Service Procedures	服务程序要点
Before Take-off	（1）Guide passengers. （2）Confirm emergency exit passengers and report to purser. （3）The purser shall confirm and close the cabin door, report to the captain. （4）Operate the cabin door to “armed” position and report. （5）Show safety demonstration. （6）To meet the needs of passengers, such as newspapers, blankets, etc., before taxiing. （7）Pre-take-off safety check/specific guidance for special passengers. （8）Safety confirmation of cabin crew.	（1）迎客/疏导旅客/整理行李架。 （2）确认应急出口情况并报告乘务长。 （3）乘务长进行关舱门前各项确认，报告机长，关机门。 （4）得到乘务长广播指令后对照《舱门操作检查单》操作舱门预位，并报告。 （5）观看安全示范录像或人工安全示范表演。 （6）在飞机滑行前随时满足旅客需求，如报纸、毛毯等。 （7）起飞前安全检查/对特殊旅客进行针对性的指导。 （8）乘务员自身安全确认。

续表

Phase of flight	Service Procedures	服务程序要点
After Take-off	（1）Open the toilets at cruising level or 20 minutes after take-off. （2）Provide newspapers and blankets. （3）Provide headphones and amenity kits. （4）Drink service. （5）Meal tray service. （6）Drink refilling after meal service. （7）Waste collection. （8）Coffee and tea service. （9）Provide entry cards to passengers. （10）Duty free sales. （11）Crew rest/lavatory cleaning/drink service on demand/bar service. （12）Provide hot towels. （13）Drink and meal service for the second round. （14）Provide the membership application forms if necessary. （15）Complete the quarantine announcement 40 minutes before landing. （16）Complete the immigration announcement 35 minutes before landing. （17）Safety check 30 minutes before landing. Safety confirmation of cabin crew.	（1）"系好安全带指示灯"熄灭后或起飞后 20 分钟，打开卫生间。 （2）细微服务。 （3）耳机服务、洗漱包服务（如有）。 （4）饮料服务。 （5）餐食服务。 （6）添加饮料服务。 （7）回收垃圾。 （8）茶水、咖啡服务。 （9）为有需要的旅客提供入境卡，并协助旅客进行填写。 （10）免税品销售。 （11）值班、轮休、吧台服务、巡舱、细微服务及卫生间打扫。 （12）热毛巾服务。 （13）落地前 3 小时左右，提供二餐服务。 （14）若有旅客需要，及时送上会员申请表。 （15）国际/地区航线入境航班在落地前 40 分钟进行入境健康检疫广播。 （16）落地前 35 分钟完成入境广播词。 （17）落地前 30 分钟进行下降前安全检查广播，完成各自区域安全检查，及时归位。
Landing	（1）Monitor the cabin to prevent passengers from standing up when taxiing. （2）Operate the cabin door to "Disarmed" position and report. （3）Open the cabin door according to purser's instruction. （4）Carry out entry formalities with immigration officers. （5）Disembarkation of the passengers. （6）Check cabin. （7）Report to purser.	（1）监控责任区域，制止旅客站起来整理行李。 （2）得到乘务长广播指令后对照《舱门操作检查单》操作舱门解除预位，并报告。 （3）得到乘务长指令后开舱门。 （4）与边检人员进行入境手续交接。 （5）送客。 （6）清舱。 （7）报乘务长。

第二节　国际航班乘务员机上工作专业术语

一、常见特殊餐食代码及介绍

常见特殊餐食代码及介绍详见表 1-2-10。

表 1-2-10　常见特殊餐食代码及介绍

Special Meal Code	Full Name of the Special Meal	餐食特点
BBML	Baby/Infant Meal	婴儿餐是适用于二周岁以下的婴儿的餐食。
CHML	Child Meal	儿童餐是适用于二至十二周岁的儿童的餐食。
HNML	Hindu Meal	印度(教)餐是根据印度人的宗教信仰及饮食习惯制作的非素食餐。
KSML	Kosher Meal	犹太餐购自有犹太餐制作资质及信誉认证的制造商，根据犹太人宗教律法和饮食习惯制作餐食并提供服务。
MOML	Muslim Meal	穆斯林餐具有穆斯林餐食生产资质认证，是根据穆斯林的宗教律法和饮食习惯制作的餐食。
BLML	Bland Meal	清淡餐餐食为软质，低脂肪，低纤维，不含刺激性食材。
DBML	Diabetic Meal	糖尿病餐是适合糖尿病人食用的餐食，不含任何种类的糖。
LFML	Low Fat Meal	低脂低胆固醇餐使用低胆固醇、高纤维的材料，无红肉、油炸及高脂肪的餐食。
LSML	Low Salt Meal	低盐餐限制使用含有天然盐分和钠的加工食材，是不添加盐分的餐食。
GFML	Gluten Intolerant Meal	无麸质餐是不含任何形式的麸质的餐食。

续表

Special Meal Code	Full Name of the Special Meal	餐食特点
FPML	Fruit Platter Meal	水果餐是配备新鲜水果的餐食，水果种类根据供应及季节 而定。
RVML	Raw Vegetarian Meal	生鲜蔬果餐是配备新鲜水果和蔬菜的餐食，蔬果种类根据供应及季节而定。
SFML	Seafood Meal	海鲜餐包括一种或多种海鲜，是不含其他肉类制品的餐食。
LQML	Liquid Meal	流质餐主要为细小的流体食材，如奶、滤粥或清汤。
AVML	Asian Vegetarian Meal	亚洲素食印度风味素食餐,口味通常辛辣，无肉类、海鲜及鸡蛋类食材，可能包含少量乳制品。
VGML	Vegetarian Meal	西式素食餐，不含肉类、海鲜、蛋类及乳制品食材。

二、机上常见特殊旅客代码

机上常见特殊旅客代码详见表 1-2-11。

表 1-2-11　机上常见特殊旅客代码

Special Passenger Code	特殊旅客类型
MEDA	患病旅客
BLND	失明旅客/盲人
DEAF	聋哑旅客
WCHR（R: RAMP 停机坪）	轮椅旅客，旅客能够自行上下飞机，在客舱内能自己走到座位上去
WCHS（S: STEPS 台阶）	轮椅旅客，旅客不能自行上下飞机，但在客舱内能自己走到座位上去
WCHC（C: CABIN SEAT 客舱座位）	轮椅旅客，旅客完全不能走动，需要他人帮助才能进入客舱座位
STCR	担架旅客
UMNR	无人陪伴儿童
INFANT	婴儿
OXYG	需要在机上使用氧气的旅客
PREG	孕妇

三、国际航班特殊旅客代码及服务注意事项

1. 无签证过境旅客（Transit Passengers without Visas）

➢ **无签证过境旅客代码：**TWOV

➢ **服务注意事项：**

（1）无签证过境旅客不是罪犯，他们只是要通过一个他们没有获得签证的国家。

（2）无签证过境旅客可以无人陪伴旅行。除非是换飞机，否则，他们不允许在途经城市下飞机。

（3）接受和运输无签证过境旅客的航空承运人要一直负责到运送他们到离境为止，要求最后一个登机，最先一个下机。

（4）地面代理人员负责检查他们都具备到达国的所有必需文件。在航班上，装有这些文件的信封由主任乘务长/乘务长保管。负责无签证过境旅客的乘务员必须将无签证过境旅客和该信封移交给地面相关工作人员。

2. 遣返者/驱逐出境者（Deportee）

➢ **遣返者（驱逐出境者）的分类代码：**

DEPA：有人押运的遣返者

DEPU：无人押运的遣返者

➢ **遣返者服务注意事项：**

（1）被拒绝入境/遣返者（驱逐出境者）不作为囚犯运输。

（2）主任乘务长/乘务长接到当地代理人和/或边防当局的相关信息，由边防当局届时派员上机进行手续交接；主任乘务长/乘务长应将情况通报机长、空警/航空安全员。

（3）被拒绝入境/遣返者（驱逐出境者）原则上应先登机，主任乘务长/乘务长应与地面工作人员在相应单据上进行签字交接；飞机抵站后主任乘务长/乘务长应同机长、空警/航空安全员共同将被拒绝入境/遣返者（驱逐出境者）的相关证件、资料及旅客本人移交边防人员，并在乘务员、空警/航空安全员相关台账上记录交接情况。

（4）飞机上有被拒绝入境/遣返者（驱逐出境者）时，在边防人员到达之前，机上乘客不得下机。

（5）禁止向被拒绝入境/遣返者（驱逐出境者）提供含酒精的饮料和锋利的餐具；被拒绝入境/遣返者（驱逐出境者）不得被安排在出口座位就座。被运送过程中，机组人员应对被拒绝入境者（遣返旅客）实施全程安全监控。

3. 偷渡者（Stowaway）

➢ **偷渡者处理原则：**

（1）航空公司工作人员必须在他/她企图成为一个偷渡者之前判断出他/她的意图。如果一个人隐藏在任何分隔舱内，如卫生间、衣帽间、行李箱内均可被认为是偷渡者。

（2）不要试图收取他/她的费用；立即报告机长；一切可能的信息由机长通知空中交通管制部门。

（3）离港前，可要求旅客下飞机；离港后，空中交通管制负责协助并搜集有关信息向机长转达另外的指示。

思考与练习

Practice

一、简答题 Short Answer Questions

1. 请概括国际远程航班服务程序与国内航班服务程序的区别。

Please outline the difference between the service procedures for international long-distance flights and those for domestic flights.

2. 请概括国际航班遣返者（驱逐出境者）的服务要点。

Please outline the main points of the services of international deporters (deportees).

二、单选题 Single Choice Questions

1. 海鲜餐的代码是？ What's the code for the seafood meal?

A. RVML.

B. SFML.

C. AVML.

D. VGML.

2. 根据客舱安全管理规定，起飞后（　　）分钟可以开始进行客舱服务。

A. 10 分钟。

B. 15 分钟。

C. 5 分钟。

D. 20 分钟。

According to cabin safety regulations, cabin service can begin at (　　) minutes after takeoff.

A. 10 minutes.

B. 15 minutes.

C. 5 minutes.

D. 20 minutes.

单元三　国际航班预先准备阶段程序

第一节　乘务员执勤时间的相关规定

一、乘务员值勤期休息期的概念

（1）飞行时间。

飞行时间是指飞机为准备起飞而借自身动力开始移动时起，直到飞行结束停止移动为止的时间。

（2）飞行值勤期。

飞行值勤期是指机组成员接受合格证持有人安排的飞行任务后（包括飞行、调机或转场等），从为完成该次任务而到指定地点报到的时刻开始，到飞机在最后一次飞行后发动机关闭且机组成员没有再次移动飞机的意向为止的时间段。

（3）休息期。

休息期是指从机组成员到达适宜的住宿场所起，到为执行下一次任务离开适宜的住宿场所为止的连续时间段。在该段时间内，合格证持有人不得为机组成员安排任何工作和给予任何打扰。

二、乘务员的累积飞行时间及休息期限制

（1）累积飞行时间。

根据中国民航局规章，客舱乘务员管理部门不得安排乘务员的飞行任务超过民航局规定的时间限制，乘务员也不得接受超过时间限制的飞行任务。每位乘务人员应掌握自己每月的飞行时间，当发现飞行计划有可能使自己的飞行时间超出日、月、年规定的飞行时间限制时，有责任依据 CCAR-121 部要求主动报告排班部门进行调整。

根据《大型飞机公共航空运输承运人运行合格审定规则》（CCAR121-R7），客舱乘务员的累积飞行时间、值勤时间限制规定如下：

① 任一日历月，100 小时的飞行时间。

② 任一日历年，1 100 小时的飞行时间。

③ 任何连续 7 个日历日，70 小时的飞行值勤期。

④ 任一日历月，230 小时的飞行值勤期。

（2）休息期。

根据《大型飞机公共航空运输承运人运行合格审定规则》（CCAR121-R7），客舱乘务员的休息期规定如下：

任一机组成员在实施飞行任务或者主备份前的 144 小时内，航空公司应当为其安排一个至少连续 48 小时的休息期。

如果飞行值勤期的终止地点所在时区与机组成员的基地所在时区之间有 6 个或者 6 个小时以上的时差，则当机组成员回到基地以后，航空公司必须为其安排一个至少连续 48 个小时的休息期。这一休息期应当在机组成员进入下一值勤期之前安排。

除非机组成员在前一个飞行值勤期结束后至下一个飞行值勤期开始前，获得了至少连续 10 个小时的休息期，航空公司不得安排，且任何机组成员也不得接受任何飞行值勤任务。

三、乘务员酒精、药物限制

（1）依据中国民航局规章，在计划飞行的 8 小时内，任何机组人员不得饮用含酒精的饮料，机组人员呼出气体中所含酒精浓度达到或者超过 0.04 克/210 升，或者在酒精作用状态下，不得上岗值勤或者继续留在岗位上。

（2）高原机场运行时，机组人员飞行前 24 小时禁止酒精饮品，避免劳累或过量无氧运动，且有足够的睡眠。

（3）机组成员在值勤过程中，不得饮用含酒精的饮料。

（4）机组成员不得使用或携带鸦片、海洛因、甲基苯丙胺（冰毒）、吗啡、大麻、可卡因以及国家规定管制的其他能够使人形成瘾癖的麻醉药品和精神药品。

（5）在值勤前和值勤中不得使用可能造成生理异常或影响正常履行职责的药物。但经航空医师确认的不影响正常履行职责的治疗药物除外。

第二节　飞行前预先准备的内容

一、飞行前准备（Preflight Preparation）

乘务员在执行航班前一天需进行网上准备，了解最新安全规章、业务通告、航班号、飞机号、机组构成情况、航线、起飞落地时间、有无 VIP 旅客等。主任乘务长/乘务长针对航班要求进行网上留言，乘务员学习留言并根据留言要求进行飞行前准备。具体如表 1-3-1 所示。

表 1-3-1　乘务员航前个人准备要点

Cabin Crew Preparation before the Flight	乘务员航前个人准备要点
（1）Check the flight plan according to the published flight schedule.	（1）根据公布的航班计划表了解自己的飞行计划动态。
（2）Check the flight information online one day before the task, including flight information, CIQ, catering information, seat reservation information, etc.	（2）任务前一天在网上查阅航班情况，进行网上准备，并根据需要填写在记录本上，查询内容包括：航线特点、CIQ、配餐信息、定座信息等。
（3）Prepare uniforms.	（3）准备次日任务所需制服及驻外站时所需衣物用品。
（4）Confirm the validity of certificates (flight attendant training certificate, medical certificate, crew pass, etc.).	（4）确认证件（乘务员训练合格证、航空人员体检合格证、空勤登机证、危险品运输训练合格证等）在位，并处于有效期。
（5）Confirm the flight documents and goods, including Service Notice, Cabin Announcement, Cabin Door Operation Checklists, Flight Attendant Medical Certificate, watches, contact lenses, and a pair of frame lenses .	（5）确认业务资料、物品在位，包括：业务通告、《客舱广播词》、舱门操作检查单、走时准确的手表、“航空人员体检合格证”上注明有“戴矫正镜”者需佩戴角膜接触镜/视力矫正镜，并携带一副与所佩戴矫正镜度数相同的框架式矫正镜等。
（6）Review the use of emergency equipment of aircraft types.	（6）复习所飞机型的应急设备使用方法和机型常识。
（7）Get enough sleep.	（7）充足的睡眠。
（8）Comply with the regulations before flight.	（8）遵守空勤人员出任务前的有关个人作息的规定。

二、乘务组预先准备会程序（Cabin Crew Preflight Briefing）

（1）预先准备会报到时间及地点（Check in time and place for briefing）。

一般情况下，执行航班任务应在计划起飞前至少 1 小时 30 分钟到达准备地点报到，具体报到时间根据各航空公司的规定执行。具体内容详见表 1-3-2。

表 1-3-2 预先准备会内容

Cabin Crew Preflight Briefing Procedures (about 20 minutes)	**乘务组预先准备会程序**
(1) Check documents.	(1) 检查各种证件资料是否齐全（国际、地区航线由安全员领取护照）。
(2) Notify flight information: flight number, captain's name, flight time, etc.	(2) 航班号、飞机号、机长姓名、安全员姓名、航线、起飞落地时间等。
(3) Cabin crew position designation.	(3) 号位分工。
(4) Coordinate security plan with air marshal.	(4) 空警协同空防预案（包括暗语暗号、进入驾驶舱的规定、发生可疑行为和违反安全保卫事件时向飞行机组的报告方式、空防安全事件的处置等）。
(5) Review emergency responsibilities and procedures plan.	(5) 乘务长提问：最新安全规章、业务通告的掌握情况、正常情况下的安全规定，舱门及出口的管理与监控。
(6) Discuss inflight service and emergency cases.	(6) 应急情况下乘务员的职责、脱出区域与携带物品，应急处置程序，应急撤离程序；机上救护等。
(7) Notify service requirements and appearance requirements.	(7) 学习新的业务通告与案例。
(8) Convey important flight operation information.	(8) 提出服务要求及仪容仪表要求。
(9) Convey CIQ regulations for international and regional airlines.	(9) 传达航班重要运行信息及工作要求；国际、地区航线提问 CIQ 规定。

(2) 预先准备会结束后乘车进场（Pick up for airport）。

① The cabin crew shall wait at the bus station five minutes in advance. The pick up time is usually 1hour and 10 minutes before STD.

② Before boarding the bus, the cabin crew and the safety officer should conduct cross check of the baggage.

③ The cabin crew line up to board the plane.

三、机组协同（Crew Coordination）

飞行机组与客舱机组应加强联络和协作配合，完善和全面增强机组保证安全的能力。在飞行运行期间必须遵守各自的运行程序和职责，了解对方的工作职责、程序，熟悉对方在运行各个阶段的工作内容及考虑因素，以及工作意图和行动方案，更好地共同完成飞行任务，具体内容详见表 1-3-3。

表 1-3-3 机组协同项目及内容

机组协同项目 Crew Coordination Items	机组协同内容 Coordination Contents
1. 核对任务书。 Check the mission assignment sheet.	1.1 再次核对任务书乘务组姓名（含加机组人员），销毁多余任务书（如有），乘务长签字确认。 Recheck the names of the cabin crew member on the mission assignment sheet. Destroy the extra mission assignment sheet (if any) and ask the purser to sign.
2. 空防预案。 Inflight security contingency plan.	2.1 暗语暗号。 Password and signal. 2.2 机长明确正常情况及特殊情况（含机组失能、正常联络下无应答）进出驾驶舱的方式及特殊要求。 The ways to access into the cockpit: the captain should clarify the normal and abnormal ways to access into the cockpit and any special requirements. (Including crew incapacitation, no response from cockpit under normal conditions etc.). 2.3 发生可疑行为和违反安全保卫事件时向飞行机组的报告方式。 The way to report to cockpit crew in case of the occurrence of any suspected action and any violation event in respect of safety and security. 2.4 扰乱行为、非法干扰的处置。 The actions to be taken on any disturbance actions and illegal disturbance.
3. 颠簸。 Turbulence.	3.1 驾驶舱信号发出的方式。 The way to send signals from the cockpit. 3.2 根据飞行机组通报，了解航路天气及可能发生的颠簸。 Get information from the crew about enroute weather and possible turbulent areas.
4. 紧急撤离。 Emergency Evacuation.	4.1 明确和确认撤离信号、撤离口令、何种情况下需要撤离、发出撤离信号的权限。 Clarify and confirm the evacuation signal, evacuation call-out, and the authority to deliver the signal. 4.2 明确紧急迫降，高度在2 000英尺、500英尺及飞机停稳时，飞行机组发出的具体口令。 Clarify the call-out from cockpit crew for emergency forced landing. Call-outs from the cockpit at 2000ft, 500ft and when aircraft is stopped.

续表

机组协同项目 **Crew Coordination Items**	机组协同内容 **Coordination Contents**
5. 驾驶舱与客舱联络。 Communication between cockpit and cabin.	5.1 失火、失密、燃油泄漏、劫炸机时的报告人（第一发现者）、报告方式及时机（能否立即报告）。 Who (the first one recognize the problem) and when (immediately or any specific phase) to report abnormals like fire, depressurization, fuel leakage and hi-jacking. 5.2 应急情况下通信设备故障/系统故障时的备份联络方式。 Stand by ways to contact when there is communication equipment failure or system failure under emergency conditions. 5.3 起飞/落地前、完成客舱准备后向飞行机组报告的方式。 How to report to cockpit when cabin is secured for takeoff or landing.
6. 运行不正常情况。 Abnormal operation Conditions.	6.1 提前10分钟（含）以上到达时飞行机组对客舱机组的通知。 How to notify the cabin if the actual arrival time is 10 minutes and more ahead of schedule. 6.2 航班延误时飞行机组对客舱机组的通知。 How to notify the cabin crew in case of delay.

思考与练习

Practice

一、国际航班信息收集 International Flight Information Collection

国际航班信息策划。每组策划一个计划执飞的国际航班，并收集航班信息，使用英语完成以下 Internation Flight Information 的填写。

Each group plans an international flight and collects flight information. Complete the following “Internation Flight Information” chart in English.

International Flight Information

Flight Number	
Departure Airport （English full name and IATA code 三字代码）	
Arrival Airport （English full name and IATA code）	
Departure Time – Arrival Time	
Flight Time	
Aircraft Type	
Captain	
Route Information: ● Fly over the countries: ● Fly over the cities: ● Fly over the rivers: ● Fly over the mountains:	
Customs Immigration and Quarantine Regulations（目的地海关检验检疫信息）	
Special Passengers （at least 2 types 至少 2 类特殊旅客代码）	
Special Meals（at least 2 types）	
Service Positions of the Cabin Crew（乘务组号位分工）	

二、情景模拟 Scenario Simulation

1. 每组同学请根据国际航班预先准备会程序，使用英语完成乘务组准备会情景模拟。

Students of each group should complete the scenario simulation of cabin crew Preflight Briefing in English according to the procedure of international flight.

2. 每组参考以下《国际航班乘务组准备会考核标准》，对其他小组的准备会完成情况进行打分评价。

Each group shall score and evaluate the completion of cabin crew Preflight Briefing of other groups by referring to the following Preflight Briefing Assessment Standards.

国际航班乘务组准备会考核标准

Preflight Briefing Assessment Standards

序号	考核要点	Assessment Standards	分值	得分
1	乘务组职业化形象标准	Professional image standards for cabin crew	10	
2	准备会流程的完整性、航线资料准备充分性；国际地区证照及物品（资料）携带/自查	The completeness of the preflight briefing process and the international flight certificates self-examination	10	
3	各号位乘务员应急撤离职责的准备	Preparation of emergency evacuation duty of flight attendants at each station	10	
4	乘务员对应急设备使用方法的熟练度	Cabin crew's proficiency in using emergency equipment	10	
5	乘务组对客舱安全方面的准备（颠簸、灭火处置等）	Cabin safety preparation of cabin crew (turbulence, fire fighting, etc.)	20	
6	乘务组对客舱服务方面的准备（服务程序、特殊旅客、特殊餐食等）	Preparation of cabin services by cabin crew (service procedures, special passengers service, special meal service, etc.)	20	
7	各组员对目的地 CIQ 的熟悉程度	Familiarity with destination CIQ	10	
8	乘务组英文流畅	Fluent English	10	
总分 Total Score				

单元四　国际航班直接准备阶段服务

第一节　应急设备检查

一、应急设备检查程序（详见表 1-4-1）

表 1-4-1　应急设备检查程序

Emergency Equipment Check Procedures	应急设备检查程序
（1）According to the airline's Cabin Crew Manual, after the crew is on duty or the aircraft is left unattended, the crew must check the emergency equipment to ensure that the cabin emergency systems and equipment are in place, accessible and usable. And report to the Chief Purser for inspection.	（1）根据航空公司的客舱乘务员手册要求，乘务组上机执勤或飞机无人看管后，乘务组必须检查责任区紧急设备，确保客舱紧急系统和设备已就位、可拿取、可使用。并报告主任乘务长/乘务长检查情况。
（2）Put the cabin attendant manuals in the special lockers for easy access.	（2）检查完毕后，将客舱乘务员手册统一放在前、中、后舱易拿取的专用储物柜内。
（3）Put the crew checklists in place.	（3）相关职责的乘务员将《舱门操作检查单》和《出口座位旅客确认流程单》放到指定位置。

二、应急设备检查报告程序

（1）After checking and verifying, report to chief purser.

（2）The chief purser reports to the captain on the inspection of emergency equipment.

（3）During operation, report to the captain before using emergency equipment. In case of emergency, handle and report at the same time.

（4）If it is found that the equipment does not affect airworthiness, report to the captain and maintenance personnel and record the problems in the Cabin Log Book.

（5）If the equipment is found missing or does not meet the operation requirements, the flight attendants shall inform the captain and maintenance personnel to deal with it in time before departure, so as to meet the operation requirements.

第二节　服务设备检查及准备

服务设备检查程序详见表 1-4-2。

表 1-4-2　服务设备检查程序

Service Equipment Check Procedures	服务设备检查程序
（1）Open all overhead bins and storage spaces for inspection, and report to chief purser.	（1）打开责任区域所有行李架及储藏空间清舱检查，并报告主任乘务长/乘务长清舱情况。
（2）Check the cabin equipment and open the ventilation holes and shades. Check the passenger entertainment system and service system, report to chief purser.	（2）检查责任区域的客舱设备，打开通风孔及遮光板；检查责任区域的旅客娱乐系统和服务系统，发现问题及时向主任乘务长/乘务长报告。
（3）Check the availability of the galley, meals, and containers or cutlery.	（3）厨房乘务员要检查机供品（餐食）情况，如果有不能打开的容器或餐具，应当向主任乘务长/乘务长报告，即使在最后一刻装上飞机的物品，也要进行检查（需要时应开箱）。
（4）If the cabin crew finds any suspicious items during the inspection, do not touch them, report to the chief purser.	（4）客舱乘务员如在检查中发现任何可疑的物品，不要触动，立即通知航空安全员处理，并同时报告主任乘务长/乘务长，主任乘务长/乘务长立即报告机长。

第三节　服务准备

一、阅读物品准备（Newspaper Preparation）

图 1-4-1　报刊服务

经济舱报纸摆放位置及服务要点详见表 1-4-3。

表 1-4-3 经济舱报纸摆放位置及服务要点

Economy Class Newspaper Setting Place	经济舱报纸摆放位置及服务要点
Galley.	在旅客登机经过的厨房服务间台面整齐摆放报纸。
The service cart at the boarding gate.	将报纸整齐摆放在廊桥口报刊车上。
Cabin crew provide newspapers on demand.	同时为多位旅客单独发放报刊，将报刊对折、整齐摆放、左手托住报刊底边拿出，面向旅客，右手递送，刊头始终对向旅客。

二、卫生间检查及整理（Lavatory Preparation）

（1）卫生间物品配置要求详见表 1-4-4。

表 1-4-4 卫生间物品配置要求

Lavatory Service Items	卫生间用品放置要点
Toilet paper	卫生纸撕去包装纸，悬挂在卫生纸固定支架上，将卫生纸的边缘折成内三角形；放于卫生用品储藏盒下端。
The box of tissue	盒抽纸将包装封口撕开，抽出纸巾一端，以平整为宜，放于卫生用品储藏盒上端。
Towels	擦手纸将包装封口撕开，抽出纸巾一端，以平整为宜。
Cushion paper	坐垫纸保留包装盒，放于卫生间壁板储藏盒内。
Hand sanitizer	确认洗手液灌入洗手液储放容器中。
Scented tablets	香片撕去包装悬挂在卫生间门板上方的物品挂钩上。

图 1-4-2　飞机卫生间设施

（2）卫生间航前检查要求详见表 1-4-5。

表 1-4-5　卫生间航前检查要求

Equipment	Lavatory Preflight Check
Smoke detector	Smoke detector works normally.
The automatic fire extinguisher	The automatic fire extinguisher is working.
Call button	The call button in the toilet works normally.
Lavatory door lock	The lavatory door lock can be used normally.
Water	Water has been filled.
Flush	The toilet flush works normally.
Cleanness	The floor, toilet, wash basin, table and mirror are clean and bright.

三、客舱整理及厨房准备(Cabin and Galley Preparation)

图 1-4-3　整理规范的客舱

（1）客舱整理详见表 1-4-6。

表 1-4-6　客舱整理要求

Normal Seat Pocket	Emergency Exit Seat Pocket
（1）Safety instruction card. （2）Airsickness bag. （3）Magazine. Note: Place from the outside to the inside of seat pocket. Safety instruction card is placed first on the outside.	（1）Safety instruction card. （2）Emergency exit information card. （3）Airsickness bag. （4）Magazine. Note: Place from the outside to the inside of seat pocket. Safety instruction card is placed first on the outside.

① Open window shades into place. Open all vents.

② Adjust the seat back to the normal position and check that there is no ground staff in the cabin.

③ Open the overhead bins and check.

④ Spray air freshener properly in the cabin.

⑤ Check sanitation of the cabin and report to the purser.

（2）厨房准备详见表 1-4-7。

表 1-4-7　厨房准备

Galley Preparation Procedures	厨房准备程序要点
（1）Safety inspection of carts (confirm lock seal and brake intact).	（1）餐车安全检查（确认锁扣铅封，刹车完好）。
（2）Check the lock number. Count the supplies in detail.	（2）核对锁扣号，根据供应单详细清点供应品，整件物品开箱检查。
（3）Count passenger and special meals according to the catering list. Confirm the quantity and variety of meals.	（3）根据配餐单详细清点机组餐食、旅客餐食、特殊餐食，确认餐食数量、品种，抽查餐食品质。
（4）Dry ice in the dining car should be properly placed to ensure the freshness of food.	（4）了解餐食数量及分布确切位置，餐车内的干冰需妥善放置以确保食物新鲜。
（5）Check all appliances.	（5）清点各项用具，如有用品短缺，立即反映以便补充。
（6）Inform all flight attendants about the provision, quantity and variety of meals. Report to chief purser.	（6）向全体乘务员通报有关餐食的配备、数量和品种等情况。向乘务长报告所配餐食的情况，并与配餐工作人员进行交接签字。
（7）Heat meals. Set up carts, prepare coffee/tea.	（7）供应品、餐食整理：烤制餐食；摆放水车/餐车，准备咖啡/茶水。冲调热饮应加入 1/4 壶矿泉水，避免热饮过烫。

第四节　旅客登机前的确认

（1）Confirm all the crew members onboard.

（2）Cabin safety inspection and service preparation are ready.

（3）Turn on the cabin lights and open all the overhead bins in economy class for passengers’ storage.

（4）The crew members’ luggage has been stored in the designated locations.

（5）Chief purser reports to captain for passenger boarding permission.

（6）The chief purser confirms to the ground staff that the cabin is ready for boarding, the passenger begins to board.

思考与练习

Practice

情景模拟 Scenario Simulation

1. 各小组根据国际航班信息，使用英语完成国际航班直接准备阶段工作程序情景模拟。

According to the information of international flights, each team completes the scenario simulation of the working procedure of the direct preparation stage of international flights in English.

2. 航班信息：CD345 由成都（CTU）飞往曼谷（BKK）的国际航班，机型 A320，16:00—18:30，请根据国际航班直接准备阶段工作标准，完成紧急设备检查、服务设备检查，进行服务用品准备及客舱整理。

Flight information: CD345 international flight, aircraft type A320, from Chengdu (CTU) to Bangkok (BKK) 16:00—18:30, please complete the emergency equipment inspection, service equipment inspection, service supplies preparation and cabin cleaning according to the work standard of the direct preparation stage of international flights.

3. 每组对照《国际航班直接准备阶段服务考核标准》，对其他小组完成情况进行打分评价。

Each group scored and evaluated the completion of other groups according to "Assessment Standards for Preparation of International Flights".

国际航班直接准备阶段服务考核标准

Assessment Standards for Preparation of International Flights

序号	直接准备工作程序要点	Assessment Standards	分值	得分
1	紧急设备（如灭火瓶、氧气瓶和 PBE、发报机、卫生防疫包）的位置，使用方法和注意事项，并能正确迅速取出和放回灭火瓶和氧气瓶。	Emergency equipment check (such as: fire bottles, oxygen bottles and PBE), and can correctly and quickly take out and put back fire bottles and oxygen bottles.	20	
2	服务设备及卫生情况（包括客舱、厨房、卫生间）的检查方法及汇报流程。	Inspection methods and reporting procedures for service equipment and sanitary conditions (including cabin, galley and toilet).	20	
3	厨房供应品的交接和物品的摆放。	Handover of galley supplies and arrangement of items.	20	

续表

序号	直接准备工作程序要点	Assessment Standards	分值	得分
4	客舱整理的内容（头片、《出口座位旅客须知卡》、遮光板、行李架、座椅前的杂志摆放、报刊的摆放、安全带、扶手等）。	Cabin arrangement (magazine placement in front of seat, newspaper placement, seat belt, armrest, etc.).	20	
5	旅客登机前准备/报告。	Passenger pre-boarding preparation/report.	20	
总分 **Total Score**				

单元五　国际航班飞行实施阶段客舱服务

第一节　旅客登机至起飞前

一、乘务员迎客规范（Passenger Welcome）

乘务员在迎客位置目视旅客眼睛，面带微笑，面对旅客站位 45 度，鞠躬 15 度（在旅客密集登机时使用点头礼），使用礼貌用语。迎客时应确保声音响亮，给旅客留下热情的第一印象。A320 系列机型乘务员在舱门处和客舱内的问候，问候声应以客舱内至少 3 排的旅客能够听到为宜。

图 1-5-1　乘务员迎客姿势

（1）Good morning/afternoon, sir/madam welcome aboard!

先生/女士，早上/下午好。欢迎乘坐本次航班.

Or: It’s nice to have you aboard ×× Airlines.

欢迎您乘坐 × × 航班机。

语境：乘务员在机舱门口迎接乘客时的问候语。

（2）Your boarding pass/card, please?

Or: May I see your boarding pass?

Or: Would you mind showing me your boarding pass?

请出示您的登机牌。

语境：帮助乘客找座位时。

（3）What's your seat number?

您的座位号是多少？

（4）Your seat is over there, 18A. The seat number is indicated along the edge of the overhead storage compartment.

您的座位在那儿，18A 座位号就标在行李架边上。

语境：告诉乘客其座位在机舱内的大体位置。

（5）Your seat is in the front/middle/rear of the cabin. The window/aisle/middle seat.

您的座位在前/中/后舱。靠窗/靠过道/在中间。

（6）I'll show you your seat.

我来为您引位。

语境：遇行动不方便的乘客时。

（7）This way, please.

Or: Step this way, please.

Or: Come with me, please.

Or: Follow me, please.

请随我来。

语境：同上句。

（8）May I help you with your bag?

我帮您拿行李好吗？

语境：为乘客引位时，帮其拿行李。

（9）Could you please step aside to allow other passengers to pass through?

您能往边上站一点让其他旅客过去吗？

语境：当有乘客挡住过道时。

（10）You should be seated to the assigned seat in order to ensure proper weight and balance for the aircraft when it takes off.

Or: You should take your assigned seat, for the plane must keep its balance when it takes off.

为了使飞机在起飞时保持配载平衡，请您按指定的座位入座。

语境：当有些乘客不按指定座位入座时。

（11）Could you please take the seat according to your seat number?

您能按座位号入座吗？

（12）I' m afraid you are in the wrong seat.

恐怕您坐错位了。

语境：用以提醒那些不知道自己坐错位的乘客。

二、进行客舱安全监控（Cabin Safety Monitoring）

（1）Cabin Crew should monitor the emergency exit at any time during boarding.

（2）If any passengers are not suitable for boarding, report to chief purser.

（3）If the luggage is too large to be placed on board, the chief purser should be reported in time.

（4）Report to chief purser in case of any luggage that does not comply with cabin safety regulations.

三、行李放置（Baggage Storage）

旅客登机后，乘务员要热情、礼貌引导旅客入座；协助旅客安放好行李。提醒旅客小心保管贵重及易碎物品；提醒旅客行李最好放置在视线范围内。代旅客存放的行李（大件物品）应告知旅客位置及交接方法。

（1）Your bag is too bulky and won't fit into the overhead compartment. It might fall down in case of turbulence and hurt somebody.

您的行李太笨重了，放在行李架上不合适，万一飞机颠簸掉下来，会砸伤人的。

Or: Your bag is far too heavy. If we ran into some turbulence, it might easily fall out of the rack and hurt someone.

或者：您的行李太重，如果我们遇上颠簸，很容易掉下来砸伤人的。

语境：告诉乘客其行李不宜放在行李架上。

（2）I'm afraid you'll have to stow/put your bag under the seat in front of you.

恐怕您要把行李放在您前面的座椅下面。

Or: Please don't put your box-in the overhead bin. It's too heavy, but it can be put under your seat.

或者：请不要把您的箱子放在行李架内。太重了，但可放在您的座椅下。

语境：让乘客将其行李从行李架上取出放在座椅下。

（3）You may not leave the baggage here. The aisle shouldn't be blocked.

Or: You can't put any baggage in the aisle as it mustn't be blocked.

您不能把行李放在这儿，过道不能堵塞。

语境：当有乘客将行李放在过道上时。

（4）Would you mind me putting your bag somewhere else?

不介意我把您的包放在其他地方吧？

语境：用于调整行李。

（5）I'll keep it for you carefully.

我会为您小心保存的。

语境：行李架已满，为乘客保存不宜挤压的物品。

四、紧急出口确认（Emergency Exit Introduction）

（1）符合紧急出口座位要求的旅客。

对话 1—您好，先生/小姐：欢迎您乘坐我们的航班！

Excuse me, Sir/Miss：Welcome aboard.

对话 2—您现在坐的是本架飞机紧急出口的座位。

Now, you are sitting next to the EMERGENCY EXIT of the aircraft.

对话 3—请注意（手势：指示出舱门上的开启方法流程图及开启装置）：除非是紧急逃生，飞行全程中请不要触碰紧急舱门上的开启设备（盖板及开启把手）。

Please do not touch the red cover (handle) under normal conditions, except in an emergency.

对话 4—坐在紧急出口座位的旅客在紧急逃生情况下负责打开紧急舱门，帮助旅客从滑梯撤离，请问您愿意吗？

Are you willing to open the emergency exit and help other passengers during evacuation?

对话 5—（如愿意）谢谢！接下来我将向您介绍紧急舱门的开启方法。

Thank you! I will show you how to open the emergency exit.

（备注：介绍开启方法时，客舱乘务员的手势可与步骤同步，以便旅客更直观地掌握。介绍时为避免误碰，乘务员手势与舱门上的开启设备须保持一定距离。注意不能让旅客触碰开启设备。）

（A319/320）机翼出口的开启方法：取下盖板，观察外部情况，将手柄向下拉，将紧急舱门取下扔到外面，待滑梯自动充气完毕后，帮助旅客从滑梯撤离。

Remove the handle cover; Make sure it's safe outside, pull down the control handle. The emergency exit door moves inward; Throw out the emergency exit door. When the inflation of the slide has finished, please help other passengers to evacuate.

撤离时应听从机组人员的指挥，禁止携带任何行李。但再次向您强调，除非是紧急逃生，飞行全程中请不要触碰紧急舱门上的开启设备（盖板及开启把手）（语气要强调），如旅客意外打开舱门需要承担相应法律责任。如有任何疑问，请随时向我提出来。

Please follow the instruction of the flight crew in case of emergency and do not take any baggage with you. Please do not touch the red cover (handle) under normal conditions, except in an emergency. Any passenger who opens the emergency exit by accident will bear a legal liability. If you have any question, please contact us.

对话 6—（取出并递上《出口座位须知卡》）请您在起飞前仔细阅读这张《出口座位须知卡》，如有任何疑问，请随时向我提出来。

Please read this card carefully. If you have any questions, please contact us.

对话 7—在通道、座位下及空位上不要放置任何行李物品，不可将衣物挂置在出口座位处，在整个飞行过程中务必保持应急出口的全程畅通。

No baggage can be put in the aisle or under your seat.

对话 8—请问我的介绍您清楚了吗？

Do you understand my instruction?/Are you clear?

对话 9—（客舱乘务员可抽问以下问题以确保旅客完全明白出口确认内容）

➢ 请问什么情况才能开启紧急舱门？

In what kind of situation can you open the emergency exit?

➢ 请问紧急舱门的开启方式是怎样的？

How to open an emergency exit?

➢ 请问紧急逃生时，应帮助旅客从哪里撤离？

Where do you evacuate from during an emergency?

对话 10—非常感谢您的协助/谢谢您的合作！祝您旅途愉快！

Thank you for your cooperation/help! Wish you a pleasant trip!

（2）不符合出口座位的旅客。

对话 1—您好，先生/小姐：欢迎您乘坐我们的航班！

Excuse me, Sir/Miss: Welcome aboard.

对话 2—因为您坐的是本架飞机紧急出口的座位，在特殊情况下需要您协助我们，帮助其他旅客撤离。但是由于语言的原因，您无法和他们正常沟通，因此我不得不给您换一个座位。

Now, you are sitting next to the EMERGENCY EXIT of the aircraft. In case of emergency, we need you to help us in order to insure a better evacuation. If you can not communicate with the other passengers normally, we have to change another seat for you.

对话 3—谢谢您的合作！祝您旅途愉快！

Thank you for your cooperation! We wish you a pleasant trip!

五、上客间隙细微服务(Service during Boarding)

图 1-5-2　乘务员细微服务

乘务员为旅客发放毛毯、开关阅读灯、开关通风孔。注意添补、整理一些报纸、杂志分别整齐放于杂志盒内（有杂志盒的机型），报头、刊头露出，供旅客取阅。根据客舱亮度，在发送阅读物的同时，征询旅客意见后将阅读灯打开。

（1）Our flying time should be approximately 3 hours. So we should be arriving at Guangzhou Baiyun Airport at about 11:30 a.m.

我们的飞行时间大约 3 小时。大约上午 11:30 到达广州白云机场。

语境：当乘客问及空中飞行时间及预计抵达时间时。

（2）The distance from Beijing to Tokyo is 2,113 kilometers.

北京到东京的飞行距离为 2 113 千米。

语境：当乘客问及空中飞行距离时。

（3）You can turn the knob here in whichever direction you like, or you can shut it off by turning it tightly to the right.

您可以随意转动这个（空调）把手，或者往右拧紧，把它关掉。

语境：介绍空调把手的使用方法时。

（4）This button turns on your overhead light.

这个按钮用来打开您头顶上的（阅读）灯。

语境：用以向乘客介绍座位上方按钮的功用。

（5）This one is the call button, if you need us for anything，please push it.

这是呼唤铃，如果需要我们帮忙，请按一下。

语境：用以向乘客介绍座位上方按钮的功用。

六、特殊旅客服务(Special Passenger Service)

The flight attendant shall complete the handover of special passengers with the chief purser and provide follow-up services.

（1）Consult passengers' needs in advance during the boarding process.

（2）Inform the special passengers.

（3）Introduce flight safety information, cabin layout and service equipment to special passengers.

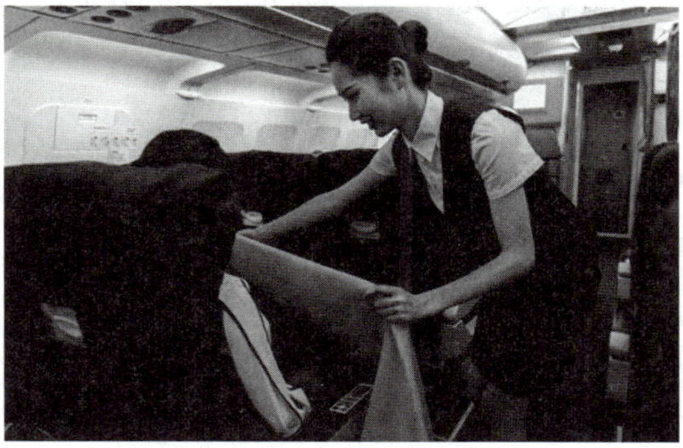

图 1-5-3　特殊旅客服务

七、关舱门后安全服务程序（Service after Door-Close）

（1）乘务长下达滑梯预位指令后，乘务员按照《舱门操作检查单》进行滑梯预位操作。

（2）安全须知演示/表演。

（3）责任区域进行起飞前安全检查：

① Would you please return to your seat? The plane is taking off soon.

请您回到您座位上好吗？飞机马上要起飞了。

语境：当飞机即将起飞时，有乘客还在过道上走动。

② Would you please return your seat back to the upright position? Just press the button on your armrest.

请您把椅背放直好吗？只要按一下您扶手上的按钮。

语境：为了乘客的安全，提醒乘客将椅背放直。

③ Please stay in your seat and keep your seat belt fastened until the sign has been turned off.

Or: Please check to see if your seat belt is fastened.

请在安全带信号熄灭前坐在座位上，系好安全带。

或者：请检查一下您的安全带是否系好。

语境：起飞前提醒乘客系好安全带。

④ Slip the belt into the buckle and pull tightly, that’s all.

把带子穿进带扣，然后抽紧，就这样。

语境：告诉乘客如何使用安全带。

⑤ The use of the lavatory has been suspended during take off.

在飞机起飞期间，卫生间暂停使用。

语境：有乘客在飞机即将起飞前要上洗手间时。

⑥ The plane is about to take off. P1ease don’t walk about in the cabin.

飞机马上要起飞了，请不要在客舱内走动。

Or: It’s dangerous to walk about during take-off,

或者：飞机起飞时，来回走动很危险。

语境：飞机起飞前有乘客在客舱内走动时。

（4）安检后归位。

① 安全检查完毕后乘务组及时回座位就座，系上安全带、肩带。

② 监控所有旅客已在座位坐好。

③ 默想紧急撤离程序。

图 1-5-4　乘务员坐姿

第二节　飞机起飞后

一、起飞后细微服务（Passenger Care Service after Take-off）

图 1-5-5　细微服务

起飞后细微服务内容详见表 1-5-1。

表 1-5-1　细微服务内容

Passenger Care Service after Take-off	**细微服务内容**
（1）Adjust air vents for passengers in need. （2）Ask and help turn on the reading light. （3）Provide blankets and newspaper. （4）Monitor cabin temperature and report to purser for adjustment.	（1）为需要的旅客调节通风口。 （2）询问并帮助打开阅读灯。 （3）发放毛毯和报纸。 （4）了解客舱温度情况，需要调节时及时报告乘务长，由乘务长进行调节。

二、起飞后饮料服务（Beverage Service）

（1）饮料服务时间及要点。

① About 20 minutes after take-off, provide drink service to passengers.

② Suspend cabin service in case of turbulence.

饮料服务要点详见表 1-5-2。

表 1-5-2　饮料服务要点

Non-Alcoholic Beverages	Service Methods
Fruit juice: orange juice, tomato juice, etc.	Ready to be served chilled after mixing with ice.
Coke, 7-up, tonic, soda, ginger ale (dry)	Served chilled with ice and/or mixed with alcoholic beverages.
Coffee	Served very hot with sugar and cream or condensed milk.
Tea	Served hot with meal.

图 1-5-6　机上饮料服务

（2）饮料服务标准英语对话。

① Would you like something hot/cold to drink?

您想来点热/冷饮料吗？

We have iced water, orange squash, Coca Cola, 7-up and so on. Which do you prefer?

我们有冰水、橘子汁、可口可乐、七喜等，您喜欢哪一种？

语境：在饮料供应时，为乘客提供多种饮料选择。

② Coffee isn’t ready yet, would you like to have a cup of hot tea instead?

咖啡还未冲好，来杯热茶好吗？

语境：当乘客所要的饮料暂时没有时。

③ Would you like me to refill your coffee/tea?

您要不要再添些咖啡/茶？

语境：主动为乘客添加饮料时。

④ Would you like some ice in your drink?

您想在饮料里放点冰块吗？

语境：同上句。

⑤ It's hot! Mind your hand.

小心烫手！

语境：提供热饮料时。

⑥ Would you care for some wine with your meal?

您想来点随餐酒吗？

语境：为乘客提供酒类服务。

⑦ Would you like your whisky straight or on the rocks?

您喜欢威士忌直饮还是加冰块？

三、餐食服务（Meal Service）

餐食服务注意事项详见表 1-5-3。

表 1-5-3　餐食服务注意事项

Meal Service Methods	餐食服务要点
（1）Flight attendants serve passengers on their right hand first, then passengers on their left.	（1）原则上乘务员先为自己右手边的旅客服务，再为左手边的旅客服务。
（2）Introduce the name of the dish (such as mushroom chicken rice). Meal tray and hot meal should be delivered at the same time.	（2）送餐饮时客舱服务区域之间也应互相协调、补充。正餐航段选餐时，应按照配备的餐食品种介绍菜名（如回锅肉米饭、香菇鸡肉米饭、双椒碎肉面）。正餐服务时餐盘与热食应同时送出，并适时提供开胃菜给旅客选用。
（3）Passengers booking or requiring special meals should be satisfied in advance.	（3）有交接单的特殊旅客、预订或需要特殊餐食的旅客及提出餐食需要的个别旅客应提前满足。

（1）经济舱正餐（Hot Meal Service in Economy Class）。

图 1-5-7　国际航班经济舱正餐

经济舱正餐服务要点详见表 1-5-4。

表 1-5-4　经济舱正餐服务要点

Hot Meal Meal Service Methods	经济舱正餐服务要点
（1）Serve as a whole tray. If there are more than two kinds of hot meal, heat for 15—20 minutes.	（1）整盘送出，如有两种（含）以上热食（烘烤 15~20 分钟），需要提前了解热食种类，以便发放及回答旅客问询。
（2）If there is any cake (bake 5—10 minutes), put it in bread basket, provide it with bread clip.	（2）在餐饮供应期间，如有蛋糕（烘烤 5~10 分钟），摆放在食品篮内（面包篮需要垫上垫纸），用面包夹发放，递给旅客手中或方型热点盒中。
（3）Sleeping passengers' rest cards will be pasted or records will be made, and flight attendants will remind each other.	（3）对睡觉旅客，视情况发放餐盒/小食品/矿泉水，粘贴休息卡或做好记录，乘务员之间相互提醒。正餐航班应等旅客醒后，及时送上餐盒与热食；已知因睡眠或其他原因放弃用餐的旅客，应及时通知其他乘务员。
（4）When the choice of meals is insufficient, it should be explained to the passengers and get understanding.	（4）主食的选择不足时，应向旅客解释并积极取得谅解。
（5）Passengers who have not slept but have given up meals should be provided with drinks at all times.	（5）未入眠但放弃用餐的旅客，应随时供应其所需的饮料。
（6）The empty meal carts should be moved back to the galley and locked.	（6）空餐车应推回厨房归位、锁定。

图 1-5-8　经济舱早餐

（2）经济舱正餐服务用语：

① What would you like to have? Roasted beef or smoked ham?

您想要吃什么？烤牛肉还是熏火腿？

语境：请乘客点菜时。

② What would you like to order for lunch?

您午餐点些什么菜？

③ I'd suggest the beef with tomatoes.

我建议您点番茄牛肉。

语境：当乘客拿不定主意点什么菜时。

④ Our meals on board are designed to meet both Chinese and Western tastes.

我们机上配备的餐食既有中式口味也有西式口味。

⑤ Are you a vegetarian? We can serve you a vegetarian meal. Would that be all right, sir?

您是位食素者吗？我们可以给您提供素食。先生，您要不要来点？

语境：为食素者提供餐食服务。

⑥ I'm sorry. There is no more fish left. Can you make a change? We have chicken. Would you like some?

对不起，鱼肉没有了。您能换一道菜吗？我们有鸡肉，您想来点吗？

Or: I'm afraid we have run out of fish. Would you like to try something else?

或者：不好意思鱼肉已发完了。您愿意尝尝别的菜吗？

语境：乘客点的菜已用完时。

⑦ Your chicken will be ready in a few minutes.

您的鸡肉几分钟后就好。

语境：乘客问及何时上菜时。

⑧ I'm very sorry for the mistake. I'll change it for you at once. Please wait a moment.

真是十分抱歉，我弄错了。我马上给您换一份，请稍候。

语境：将乘客所点的餐饮上错时。

（3）经济舱点心餐服务用语（Light Meal Service）。

图 1-5-9 经济舱点心餐

① May I offer you some refreshments, sir?

先生来点点心吗？

② Sorry, sir. This is a short flight. We only serve beverages and refreshments.

对不起，先生。这是短途航线，我们只供应饮料和点心。

语境：当乘客问及何时供餐时。

③ We have cold and hot drinks, biscuits, cream, and cakes. What would you like to have?

我们有冷、热饮料，饼干，奶油蛋糕，您喜欢吃什么？

语境：告诉短途航线上的乘客不供餐之后。

四、餐盘回收及客舱整理（Waste Collection）

图 1-5-10 回收垃圾服务

（1）Have you finished eating, sir? May I clear your table?

先生您用完餐了吗？我可以清理小桌板了吗？

语境：为乘客清理小桌板前。

（2）Would you mind me taking these away?

您介意我把这些东西拿走吗？

语境：同上句。

（3）It's my pleasure to be at your service.

为您服务是我的荣幸。

五、免税品销售用语（Duty Free Sales）

（1）Would you like to buy some duty free items?

您买点机上的免税商品吗？

语境：在机上销售免税商品时。

（2）I' m sorry, sir. We don't accept...You have to pay for it in US, Australian, New Zealand and HK dollars.

对不起，我们不收……（这种货币）我们只收美元、澳元、新西兰元、港币。

（3）Here is your change, sir. Thank you very much.

先生，这是找您的零钱，谢谢。

语境：找乘客零钱时。

六、提供入境卡（Entry Card Service）

（1）In order to speed up the arrival formalities in the destination airport, you're requested to fill in the forms for the Customs，Immigration and Quarantine before landing.

为了尽快办好到达目的地机场的手续，需要您在着陆之前填写好有关海关、移民、检疫的表格。

Or: Would you please fill out these forms before you get to Shanghai? You'll need them when you go through Immigration, Customs and Quarantine.

或者：请您在到达上海之前填写好这些表格。当您在办理移民、海关和检疫等手续时需要它们。

语境：到达目的地机场前，让乘客填写各种入境表格时。

（2）Please don’t hesitate to call us if you have any questions or difficulties in filling out these forms. We shall be more than happy to assist.

填写这些表格时，如有任何问题或困难，请随时叫我们。我们会非常乐意协助您的。

七、值班、轮休、吧台服务（Service after First Meal）

（1）值班期间的细微服务详见表 1-5-5。

表 1-5-5 值班期间的细微服务

Service after First Meal	值班期间的细微服务
（1）After the catering service, the flight attendants shall patrol the cabin to observe the needs of passengers.	（1）餐饮服务完毕后，在飞机没有出现持续颠簸的情况时应保持不间断有乘务员巡视客舱，主动观察旅客需求，要求每两排停留观察时间要达到 2~3 秒，主动及时地为旅客提供服务。
（2）Communication services. Each flight attendant should communicate with passengers for no less than 3 times.	（2）交流服务。沟通交谈时间在 3 分钟以上应采用蹲式服务，每一名乘务员在每个航班中和旅客沟通交流的次数不少于 3 人次，主任乘务长/乘务长应做好监控。
（3）When crew is cleaning lavatory:	（3）整理卫生间，保持整洁。卫生间清理时应做到：
① Explain to passengers “please wait for cleaning”.	① 向旅客说明“需要清理，请稍等”。
② When cleaning, the toilet door will be left unsealed.	② 清理时，将卫生间门虚掩，做到“四净一亮”。
③ After cleaning, toilet paper should be folded into an triangle shape.	③ 清理后，普通舱可将马桶盖内外盖全部打开；卫生纸折成内三角；盒纸、擦手纸以平整为宜。普通舱随时清理，最多不超过三人次使用。做到“四净一亮”。
（4）During night flight, cabin attendants should dim cabin light, adjust cabin temperature, so that passengers can get a better rest.	（4）夜航、长航线或大多数旅客休息时，客舱乘务员应通过“调暗客舱亮度、调节客舱温度、减少广播（分舱）、降低声音、控制音量”等方法为旅客营造良好的休息环境，让其得到更好的休息。

（2）国际航班一餐后广播。

女士们、先生们：

本架飞机将在北京时间 ×× 点 ×× 分，×× 时间 ×× 点 ×× 分到达 ×× 机场。我们

将在北京时间 × × 点 × × 分为您提供第二餐（午餐/晚餐/早餐），为了给您创造一个良好的休息环境，我们将调暗客舱灯光，请您关闭遮阳板。如果您有任何需要，请与客舱乘务员联系。谢谢！

Ladies and Gentlemen,

We will be landing at ×× airport at ×× Beijing time , ×× the local time. We will start serving the second meal (lunch/dinner/breakfast) at ×× Beijing time. For your convenience, we will dim the light, please put down the window shade. If you need any help, contact our flight attendant. Thank you!

（3）乘务员轮休注意事项详见表 1-5-6。

表 1-5-6　乘务员轮休注意事项

Crew Rest Procedures	乘务员轮休程序
（1）For flights of more than 6 hours, after the first meal, crew rest can be arranged by the chief purser.	（1）飞行时间超过 6 小时的航班，供应第一餐结束后或免税品出售完毕后可在主任乘务长/乘务长的安排下轮流值班。
（2)The flight attendants shall be on duty during the flight except for performing safety duties and completing normal service procedures.	（2）乘务员在飞行中除履行安全职责及完成正常服务程序以外的时间均应保证有人值班。
（3）Duty rotation time shall be reasonably arranged by the chief purser.	（3）值班轮换时间由主任乘务长/乘务长负责根据航班飞行时间合理安排。
（4）When on duty, the flight attendants shall monitor the safety of the cabin and provide services.	（4）值班时，乘务员需在所负责区域做好客舱监控，每 10 分钟值班员需对客舱进行安全监控及细微服务。
（5）The purser can make the flight attendant duty list according to the flight time.	（5）乘务长可根据当日航班情况制定乘务员值班表。
（6）The on-duty crew shall be at least half of the flight attendants assigned to the aircraft type.	（6）轮值班人员至少为该机型定员编制飞行人员的一半，且每个舱位的值班人数至少为该舱位的一半。
（7）There must be a purser on duty.	（7）轮值班员中，必须有一位主任乘务长/乘务长负责管理。
（8）Wake up the next shift staff 10 minutes before the end of rest. Sign the “Flight Attendant Shift Sheet” for confirmation.	（8）时间结束前 10 分钟，适时叫醒下一轮值班人员。人员进行交接时，应对机上安全工作及服务工作进行交接，并在《乘务员轮班表》上签字确认。

（4）吧台服务要点详见表 1-5-7。

表 1-5-7　吧台服务要点

Bar Service Procedures	吧台服务要点
（1）Provide bar service after the first meal service. Put all kinds of drinks and snacks in advance for passengers to choose when serving at the bar. （2）Place coffee, tea, all kinds of drinks and cups in a clear plastic drawer, and place them on the bar. （3）Arrange the snacks neatly in the bread basket and side by side with the drink drawer. （4）Hot drinks (hot water, coffee, tea, etc.) must be provided by the cabin attendant.	（1）在两餐之间为旅客提供吧台服务。相应号位客舱乘务员提前摆放各类饮品、小食品，供旅客在吧台服务时选择。 （2）乘务员将咖啡包杯、茶包杯、各种饮料酒水、纸杯由低到高、整齐有序地摆放在铺有干净垫纸的透明塑料筐内，平稳地放置在吧台上。 （3）将小食品整齐摆放在面包篮内，与饮料筐并排摆放。 （4）吧台自助服务期间，值班乘务员需做好监控。旅客需要热饮（热水、热咖啡、热茶等）时，须由客舱乘务员提供。避免因操作不当，出现安全隐患。

八、第二餐服务（The Second Meal Service）

图 1-5-11　餐饮服务

（1）Under normal circumstances, passengers are provided with the second meal about 3 hours before landing.

（2）The service standard is as the first meal service.

第三节　飞机下降

一、入境检疫广播及灭虫程序（Quarantine Procedures）

（1）入境广播。

① Quarantine announcements for international flights should be made 40 minutes before landing.

② Complete the immigration announcement 35 minutes before landing.

③ Make safety check announcements 30 minutes before landing and complete safety check in cabin.

（2）检疫用语：

According to the regulations of China/the United States...quarantine, you can't bring in fresh fruit. You have to dispose of them or give them to us before landing.

根据中国/美国……检疫的规定，您不能把新鲜水果带入境内。您必须在落地前把它们处理了或交给我们乘务员。

语境：当发现有乘客带水果去异国或带水果入境时。

二、澳洲航线灭虫程序(Spraying of Cabin)

执行飞往澳大利亚的国际航班时，乘务员应在指定时机，使用指定药物对指定区域进行喷洒。

图 1-5-12　下降前杀虫

（1）起飞前灭虫程序详见表 1-5-8。

表 1-5-8 起飞前灭虫程序

Spraying before Boarding	起飞前灭虫程序
（1）PRESRAY insecticide should be sprayed before boarding. （2）Before spraying, close the rear door and ventilation hole. Open overhead bins. Open the vent 5 minutes after spraying. （3）Spraying location: ➢ Galley, aisle, toilets and coatrooms (spraying time for each area shall not be less than 2 seconds). ➢ Crew seat, cockpit (spraying time in each area shall not be less than 3 seconds). ➢ Overhead bins and ceiling (spray time for each row of seats shall not be less than 1 second).	（1）供应配备完成后，旅客登机前喷洒 PRESRAY 杀虫剂（起飞前喷洒）。 （2）喷洒药物前，关闭后舱门及通风孔；打开行李架和通道上的储物柜；药物喷洒完五分钟后，方可打开通风孔。 （3）喷洒位置：厨房、通道、厕所、衣帽间（每一区域喷洒时间不得低于两秒）；乘务员座席、驾驶舱（每一区域喷洒时间不得低于三秒）；行李架与天花板交界处（每排座位喷洒时间不得低于一秒）。
（4）The empty bottles sprayed must be kept on the aircraft and handed over to the local officer upon arrival.	（4）喷洒完毕的空药瓶须保留在飞机上，抵达澳洲后交给当地 DAFF 官员。

（2）下降前灭虫程序详见表 1-5-9。

表 1-5-9 下降前灭虫程序

Spraying before Descent	下降前灭虫程序
（1）Spray after completing the safety check before descent. Spray TOP OF DESCENT insecticides.	（1）确保安全的前提下，完成下降前安全检查后喷洒药物。喷洒 TOP OF DESCENT 杀虫剂（下降前喷洒）。
（2）Broadcast before spraying. Close the overhead bins.	（2）喷洒药物前进行广播；喷洒药物前关闭行李架。
（3）Spraying position: ① When the flight attendant faces passengers towards the rear of the cabin, spray the junction between the seat and the floor. ② When the flight attendant faces the cockpit towards the front of the cabin, spray the junction between the overhead bins and the ceiling (spray time for each row of seats should not be less than 1 second).	（3）喷洒位置：乘务员面向旅客走向机尾时，喷洒座椅与地板交界处；背向旅客走向机头时喷洒行李架与天花板交界处（每排座位喷洒时间不得低于一秒）。

续表

Spraying before Descent	下降前灭虫程序
(4) Before opening the cabin door after landing, chief purser shows the empty cans of spray to quarantine officer as required. (5) Note: the green bottle is used for spraying before take-off, and the blue bottle is used for spraying before descent.	(4) 落地后打开舱门前主任乘务长隔着玻璃向澳方检疫官员出示喷雾剂空罐，根据澳洲检疫官员要求上交空罐。 (5) 注：绿色瓶体药物用于起飞前喷洒，蓝色瓶体药物用于下降前喷洒。

三、飞机下降安全服务工作(Safety Check before Landing)

下降前安全检查问语：

(1) Our plane is ready to land now. For the sake of safety, please stay in your seat and keep your seat belt fastened.

我们正准备降落，为了您的安全，请坐在座位上，系好安全带。

语境：飞机落地前提醒乘客系好安全带。

(2) We'll arrive at Kennedy International Airport in ten minutes. The local time is 8:10 p.m.

我们十分钟后将抵达肯尼迪国际机场。当地时间晚上 8:10。

图 1-5-13　乘务员归位

第四节　飞机着陆

(1) 要求旅客在飞机未停稳前坐在座位上。

(2) 主任乘务长/乘务长下达滑梯解除预位指令后，乘务员按照《舱门操作检查单》

进行滑梯解除预位操作。

（3）接收并明确机长“滑梯已解除预位”的口令。

（4）在指定位置向旅客致谢、道别：

① Thank you for all your cooperation during our flight.

衷心感谢您在我们飞行途中给予我们的合作。

② Hope you have a nice stay in China.

预祝您在中国度过美好时光。

③ Thank you for flying with us and hope to have the pleasure of being with you again.

感谢您乘坐我们的班机，希望能有幸再次和您见面。

（5）协助老弱妇幼及需要帮助的旅客下机。

（6）检查客舱内有无遗留物品。如有遗留物品，与地面工作人员完成移交手续。如发现可疑物品不要触碰，立即报告机长、主任乘务长/乘务长、安全员，启动相关处置程序预案。

（7）旅客及全部客舱行李离机后报告乘务长清舱情况。

（8）与交接的乘务组做好交接工作。

思考与练习

Practice

情景模拟 Scenario Simulation

1. 各小组根据国际航班信息，使用英语完成国际航班飞行实施阶段工作程序情景模拟。

According to the information of international flights, each group completed the working procedure scenario simulation of the flight implementation stage of international flights in English.

2. 各小组将执行 CD123 由成都（CTU）飞往墨尔本（MEL）的国际航班，机型 A330，09:00—20:30，请根据国际航班飞行实施阶段工作程序，完成情景模拟练习。

Each group will be the cabin crew of the international flight CD123 from Chengdu (CTU) to Melbourne (MEL), aircraft type A330, 09:00—20:30, please complete the scenario simulation exercise according to the working procedure of the flight implementation stage of international flights in English.

3. 每组对照《国际航班飞行实施阶段服务考核标准》，对其他小组完成情况进行打分评价。

Each group will evaluate the completion of other groups according to "Service Assessment Standard for International Flight Implementation Phase".

国际航班飞行实施阶段服务考核标准

Service Assessment Standard for International Flight Implementation Phase

序号	飞行实施阶段服务程序要点	Assessment Standards	分值	得分
1	迎客（包括姿态、语言及对通道的疏通、旅客的帮助）。	Welcome passengers (including gesture, languages, and help passengers).	10	
2	紧急出口确认及报告。	Emergency exit confirmation and reporting.	10	
3	安全检查项目及落实（安全带、小桌板、行李架、遮光板、座椅靠背、旅客座位前行李、空座位上的安全带等）及电子设备的使用规定。	Safety inspection and implementation (seat belt, tray table, window shade, seat back, etc.) and regulations on the use of electronic equipment.	10	
4	各岗位工作分工明确及服务程序完整、流畅。	The division of work of each position is clear and the service procedure is smooth.	10	

续表

序号	飞行实施阶段服务程序要点	Assessment Standards	分值	得分
5	卫生间的监控及整理。	Monitor and clean the toilet.	10	
6	特殊旅客的识别及服务。	Identification and service of special passengers.	10	
7	国际航班检疫规定执行、下降前灭虫程序执行。	Implement international flight quarantine regulations and pest control procedures before landing.	10	
8	专业化形象保持、微笑的运用。	Professional image maintenance, keep of smile.	10	
9	英语服务语言标准。	Service English is fluent.	10	
10	服务动作规范。	Service actions are standard.	10	
总分 Total Score				

单元六　国际航班航后讲评及航线差异

第一节　航后讲评

（1）航后讲评程序详见表 1-6-1。

表 1-6-1　航后讲评程序

Post-Flight Briefing	航后讲评程序
（1） The purser shall complete the post-flight briefing 30 minutes before landing. If the meeting is not completed, all the team members shall go to the briefing room.	（1）带班乘务长在航班降落前 30 分钟完成讲评会，如遇特殊情况未完成，在飞行结束后召集全体组员回飞行准备室进行航后讲评工作。
（2）The purser will comment on the service of the flight and make a record.	（2）带班乘务长根据航班飞行实施情况对全程工作进行讲评，总结经验教训，确认乘务员是否了解讲评内容，了解乘务员是否还有反馈信息或需要沟通的事项，并做好记录，通报得分情况。
（3）After the chief purser's comments, any questions should be addressed to the chief purser.	（3）乘务员认真听取乘务长的讲评，总结经验教训。乘务长讲评完毕后，乘务员如有疑问应及时向主任乘务长/乘务长提出。
（4）The crew should leave the airport with all flight baggage and personal certificates.	（4）乘务组着装整齐，带好所有飞行装备及个人证件集体退场。组员再次确认证件在位情况。
（5）The team members shall return to rest places by designated crew bus.	（5）组员需搭乘指定的机组车回本单位或驻外指定休息场所归队。返回基地站后，需查询航班任务有无改变，了解信息公布栏有无新信息及新通告（通知），如次日有航班任务，应按规定时间在飞行准备网上进行次日航班任务的航前准备。

（2）航后讲评检查单详见表 1-6-2。

表 1-6-2　航后讲评检查单

Post-Flight Briefing Items	The Checklist of Post-Flight Briefing
Safety of the Flight 航班安全	✓ Summarize implementation of manuals and safety regulations, etc. ✓ Comment on the good or inadequate implementation of flight attendants in their work.
Service of the Flight 航班服务	✓ Professional appearance on flights. ✓ Implementation of service. ✓ Comments on the good or inadequate aspects of the flight attendants' work.
Case Study 案例总结	✓ Summarize the safety/service cases in the flight.
Security Instruction for Layover 驻外要求	✓ Give Instructions to crew of layover abroad for international flights.
Communication with All Crew 乘务组沟通	✓ Check if the flight attendant has any feedback or needs to communicate.

第二节　国际航班驻外管理规定

（1）Abide by local and foreign customs and quarantine regulations. Pay attention to etiquette, accept and cooperate with inspection of all luggage carried in and out of customs. Illegal concealment of personal belongings is strictly prohibited.

遵守当地、各国海关、边防、检疫规定，配合检查，注重礼仪，出入关时携带全部行李物品自觉接受并配合检查。

（2）Control the total amount of foreign currencies carried abroad, not exceeding the total amount of foreign currencies that can be carried locally.

控制驻外携带外币总量，不超过当地可携带总量（指海关要求申报限额以内）。用于个人驻外生活用品（如电子产品），按当地法律法规，纳入申报。禁止携带违规、违禁物品（境外）。

（3）Personal articles (such as electronic products) used abroad shall be included in the declaration according to local laws and regulations. It is forbidden to carry illegal items.

用于个人驻外生活用品（如电子产品），按当地法律法规，纳入申报。禁止携带违规、违禁物品（境外）。

（4）It is forbidden to drink alcoholic beverages and enter local bars, gambling and other places.

禁止饮用酒精饮料和进入当地酒吧、舞厅、KTV、黄、赌、毒等场所，遵守国家法律法规，杜绝打架、斗殴等违法治安管理行为，确保人身安全。

第三节　国际短程、远程航线服务差异

国际短程、远程航线服务差异详见表 1-6-3。

表 1-6-3　国际短程、远程航线服务差异

Phase of Flight	Short Range Flight	Long Range Flight
Before Take-off	（1）Guide passengers. （2）Confirm emergency exit passengers and report to purser. （3）The purser shall confirm and close the cabin door, report to the captain. （4）Operate the cabin door to “armed” position and report. （5）Show safety demonstration. （6）To meet the needs of passengers, such as newspapers, blankets, etc. before taxiing. （7）Pre-take-off safety check/specific guidance for special passengers. （8）Safety confirmation of cabin crew.	（1）Guide passengers. （2）Confirm emergency exit passengers and report to purser. （3）The purser shall confirm and close the cabin door, report to the captain. （4）Operate the cabin door to “armed” position and report. （5）Show safety demonstration. （6）To meet the needs of passengers, such as newspapers, blankets, etc. before taxiing. （7）Pre-take-off safety check/specific guidance for special passengers. （8）Safety confirmation of cabin crew.
At Cruising Level	（1）Open the toilets at cruising level or 20minutes after take-off. （2）Provide headphones, newspapers and blankets.	（1）Open the toilets at cruising level or 20minutes after take-off. （2）Provide newspapers and blankets.

续表

Phase of Flight	Short Range Flight	Long Range Flight
At Cruising Level	（3）Provide entry cards to passengers. （4）Drink service. （5）Meal tray service. （6）Drink refilling after meal service. （7）Waste collection. （8）Coffee and tea service. （9）Duty free sales. （10）Complete the quarantine announcement 40 minutes before landing. （11）Complete the immigration announcement 35 minutes before landing. （12）Safety check 30 minutes before landing. （13）Safety confirmation of cabin crew.	（3）Provide headphones and amenity kits. （4）Drink service. （5）Meal tray service. （6）Drink refilling after meal service. （7）Waste collection. （8）Coffee and tea service. （9）Provide entry cards to passengers. （10）Duty free sales. （11）Crew rest/lavatory cleaning/drink service on demand/bar service. （12）Provide hot towels. （13）Drink and meal service for the second round. （14）Provide the membership application forms if necessary. （15）Complete the quarantine announcement 40 minutes before landing. （16）Complete the immigration announcement 35 minutes before landing. （17）Safety check 30 minutes before landing. （18）Safety confirmation of cabin crew.

续表

Phase of Flight	Short Range Flight	Long Range Flight
Landing	(1) Monitor the cabin to prevent passengers from standing up when taxiing. (2) Operate the cabin door to "Disarmed" position and report. (3) Open the cabin door according to purser's instruction.	(1) Monitor the cabin to prevent passengers from standing up when taxiing. (2) Operate the cabin door to "Disarmed" position and report. (3) Open the cabin door according to purser's instruction.
Landing	(4) Carry out entry formalities with immigration officers. (5) Disembarkation of the passengers. (6) Check cabin. (7) Report to purser.	(4) Carry out entry formalities with immigration officers. (5) Disembarkation of the passengers. (6) Check cabin. (7) Report to purser.

思考与练习

Practice

一、情景模拟 Scenario Simulation

1. 各小组根据国际航班信息，使用英语完成国际航班航后讲评情景模拟。

According to the information of international flights, each group should complete the scenario simulation of post-flight briefing of international flights in English.

2. 航班信息：各小组执行 CD123 由成都（CTU）飞往墨尔本（MEL）的国际航班，机型 A330，09:00—20:30，请根据《国际航班航后讲评单》，完成航后讲评会。

Flight information: Each group will be the cabin crew of the international flight CD123 from Chengdu (CTU) to Melbourne (MEL), aircraft type A330, 09:00—20:30, please complete the post-flight briefing according to the post-flight evaluation checklist for international flights.

Post-Flight Briefing Items	The Checklist of Post-Flight Briefing
Safety of the Flight 航班安全	✓ Summarize implementation of manuals and safety regulations, etc. ✓ Comment on the good or inadequate implementation of flight attendants in their work.
Service of the Flight 航班服务	✓ Professional appearance on flights. ✓ Implementation of service. ✓ Comments on the good or inadequate aspects of the flight attendants' work.
Case Study 案例总结	✓ Summarize the safety/service cases in the flight .
Security Instruction for Layover 驻外要求	✓ Give instructions to crew of layover abroad for international flights.
Communication with All Crew 乘务组沟通	✓ Check if the flight attendant has any feedback or needs to communicate.

二、简答题 Short Answer Questions

请从飞行时间、服务程序、机型配置等方面总结国际短程航班、远程航班的主要区别，并制作成 PPT。

Please summarize the main differences between international short-distance flights and long-distance flights from the aspects of flight time, service procedures and aircraft configuration, and make a PPT.

单元七　酒类服务

国际航班常见酒类简介详见表 1-7-1。

表 1-7-1　国际航班常见酒类简介

英　文	中　文	简　介
Spirits	烈酒	Spirits characterize ethanol, the "spirit of wine" and result from distillation. Also called hard liquor. The alcohol by volume is normally above 40%.
Brandy	白兰地	Hennessy, Remy Martin, Martell Alcohol by volume: 43%
Whiskey	威士忌	Johnnie Walker, Red Label, Black Label, Chivas Regal, White Horse, Bell's Alcohol by volume: 40%
Vodka	伏特加	Straight Vodka: Smirnoff, Stolichnaya Flavored Vodka: Blauer Bison, Pertsovka Alcohol by volume: 40%
Rum	朗姆酒	Bacardi, Captain Morgan, Myers Alcohol by volume: 45%
Gin	金酒	Dutch Gin: Bols, Bokma, Henkes Dry Gin: Gordon's, Beefeater, Tanqueray, Old Tom Alcohol by volume: 40%—52%
Tequila	特吉拉（龙舌兰）	Cuervo, El Toro, Ole Alcohol by volume: 40%
Fermented Alcoholic Beverages	酿造酒	As the most natural brewed alcohol, the ingredients of fermented alcoholic beverages are grains and fruit which can remain the original flavor.
Red Wine	红葡萄酒	Red wine is made of purple grapes, such as Shiraz, Cabernet Sauvignon, Merlot, which can be found on the tag. Alcohol by volume: 10%—30%

续表

英　文	中　文	简　介
White Wine	白葡萄酒	White wine is made of green grapes, such as Chardonnay, riesling. Alcohol by volume: 12%
Champagne	香槟	Sparkling white wine or rose wine produced in Champagne area in France. Alcohol by volume: 13%
Beer	啤酒	The alcoholic beverage made by mal. Alcohol by volume: 6%—12%

第一节　烈　酒

一、白兰地（Brandy）

白兰地是以葡萄或其他水果为原料经发酵、蒸馏而得的酒。白兰地的储存时间越长，酒的品质越佳。白兰地的酒度为 43 度左右。法国是世界上首屈一指的白兰地生产国，在法国白兰地产品中，以干邑最为著名。

干邑白兰地通常以一些英文字母来表示其陈酿时间，如 V.O 为 10~12 年；V.S.O 为 12~20 年；V.S.O.P 为 20~30 年；F.O.V 为 30 年以上；Napoleon 为 40 年以上；X.O 为 50 年以上；X 为 70 年以上，等等。

干邑白兰地的名品有轩尼诗（Hennessy）、人头马（Remy Martin）、马爹利（Martell）、卡慕（Camus）等。

白兰地主要用作餐后酒，一般不掺任何其他饮料。

二、威士忌（Whisky）

威士忌是以谷物为原料经发酵、蒸馏而得的酒。世界各地都有威士忌生产，以苏格兰威士忌最负盛名。按惯例，苏格兰、加拿大两地的威士忌书写为 Whisky，其他国家和地区的威士忌书写为 Whiskey，但在美国，两者可通用。威士忌的酒度为 40 度左右。

苏格兰威士忌的名品有约翰尼·沃克（Johnnie Walker）、红方（Red Label）、黑方（Black Label）、皇家芝华士（Chivas Regal ）、白马（White Horse）、金铃（Bell's）等。

威士忌可纯饮，也可加冰块饮用，更被大量用于调制鸡尾酒和混合饮料。

威士忌服务方法详见表 1-7-2。

表 1-7-2　威士忌服务方法

不同种类	饮用方法	服务方法
Whiskey on the Rocks	加冰	在矮玻璃杯内倒入 1/5 的威士忌，再加入 1/3 的冰块。为旅客送出时，提前放好杯垫。
Whiskey Ditch	加水	在矮玻璃杯内倒入 1/5 的威士忌，再加入 1/3 的冰水。为旅客送出时，提前放好杯垫。
Neat Whiskey	纯饮	将威士忌（1/5 杯）直接为旅客送出，需提前放好杯垫。

三、伏特加（Vodka）

伏特加是以土豆、玉米、小麦等原料经发酵、蒸馏后精制而成的酒。伏特加无需陈酿，酒度为 40 度左右。

（1）纯净伏特加（Straight Vodka）。

纯净伏特加是指将蒸馏后的原酒注入活性炭过滤槽内，过滤掉杂质而得的酒，一般无色、无味。其名品有美国的斯米尔诺夫（Smirnoff）、俄罗斯的斯多里西那亚（Stolichnaya，又称红牌伏特加）、莫斯科伏斯卡亚（Moskovskaya，又称绿牌伏特加）等。

（2）芳香伏特加（Flavored Vodka）。

芳香伏特加是指在伏特加酒液中放入药材、香料等浸制而成的酒，因此带有色泽，既有酒香，又带有药材、香料的香味。其名品有波兰的蓝野牛（Blauer Bison）、俄罗斯的珀特索伏卡（Pertsovka）等。

伏特加既可纯饮，又可广泛运用于鸡尾酒的调制，常见种类详见表 1-7-3。

表 1-7-3　伏特加常见种类

中文名	英文名	配　料
螺丝刀	Screwdriver	Vodka+orange juice
血腥玛丽	Bloody Mary	Vodka+tomato juice+pepper+salt
俄罗斯人	Russian	Vodka+gin+cocoa liqueur
咸狗	Salty Dog	Vodka+grapefruit juice+salt
奇奇	Chi-chi	Vodka+pineapple juice+coconut milk
莫斯科骡子	Moscow Mule	Vodka+lime+ginger ale

四、朗姆酒（Rum）

朗姆酒是以蔗糖汁或蔗糖浆为原料经发酵和蒸馏加工而成的酒。有时也用糖渣或其他蔗糖副产品作原料。新蒸馏出来的朗姆酒必须放入橡木桶陈酿一年以上，酒度为45度左右。

朗姆酒的名品主要有波多黎谷的百加地（Bacardi）、牙买加的摩根船长（Captain Morgan）、美雅（Myers）等。

朗姆酒既可净饮，也可加冰块饮用，还可广泛用于调制鸡尾酒或混合饮料，常见种类详见表 1-7-4。

表 1-7-4　常见朗姆酒种类

中文名	英文名	配　料
莫吉托	Mojito	Rum+lemon+mint+soda water
得其利	Daiquiri	Rum+cointreau+lemon+banama
椰林飘香	Pina Colada	Rum+coconut rum+pineapple juice+coconut milk
迈泰	Mai Tai	Light rum+dark rum+orange curacao
桑比	Zombie	Rum+lemon juice+orange juice+grenadine
探戈	Tango	Bacardi rum+sweet vermouth+dry vermouth+benedictine+orange juice
新月	New Moon	Light rum+creme de banana+white creme de cacao+cherry brandy

五、金酒（Gin）

金酒又称琴酒、毡酒或杜松子酒，是以玉米、麦牙等谷物为原料经发酵、蒸馏后，加入杜松子和其他一些芳香原料再次蒸馏而得的酒。金酒无需陈酿，酒度为 40 ~ 52 度。

（1）荷兰金酒（Dutch Gin）。

荷兰金酒具有芳香浓郁的特点，并带有明显的麦芽香味，其名品有波尔斯（Bols）、宝马（Bokma）、汉斯（Henkes）等。

荷兰金酒只适宜作净饮，不能与其他酒类饮料混合以调制鸡尾酒。

（2）干金酒（Dry Gin）。

干金酒以玉米、麦芽、裸麦等为原料（其中玉米占 75%）经发酵、蒸馏后，加入杜松子及其他香料（以杜松子为主，其他香料用量较少）再次蒸馏而成。其主要产地是英国，名品有哥顿（Gordon's）、将军（Beefeater）、得其利（Tanqueray）、老汤姆（Old Tom）等。

干金酒既可纯饮，又可广泛用于调制鸡尾酒，常见种类详见表 1-7-5。

表 1-7-5　干金酒常见种类

中文名	英文名	配　料
金汤力	Gin Tonic	Gin+tonic water+lemon
布朗士	Bronx	Gin+vermouth+orange juice
吉利特	Gimlet	Gin+lime juice
黄金菲仕	Golden Fizz	Gin+lime juice+cream+egg+soda water
百万富翁	Millionaire	Gin+lemon juice+sweet vermouth+grenadine
亚历山大姐妹	Alexander Sister	Gin+green creme de menthe+cream

六、特吉拉(Tequila)

特吉拉酒产于墨西哥，是以一种被称作龙舌兰（Agave）的热带仙人掌类植物的汁浆为原料经发酵、蒸馏而得的酒。新蒸馏出来的特吉拉需放在木桶内陈酿，也可直接装瓶出售。其名品有凯尔弗（Cuervo）、斗牛士（El Toro）、欧雷（Ole）、玛丽亚西（Mariachi）等。

特吉拉酒可净饮或加冰块饮用，也可用于调制鸡尾酒。在净饮时常用柠檬角蘸盐伴饮，常见种类详见表 1-7-6。

表 1-7-6　特吉拉常见种类

中文名	英文名	配　料
日出	Tequila Sunrise	Tequila+orange juice+grenadine
尼克佳人	Nike Lady	Tequila+cointreau+lime juice
蓝色玛格丽特	Blue Margaret	Tequila+blue curacao+lime juice

第二节　酿造酒

一、红葡萄酒（Red Wine）

葡萄酒按其颜色可分为下列三种：红葡萄酒（Red Wine）、白葡萄酒（White Wine）、玫瑰葡萄酒（Rose Wine）。

红葡萄酒是以紫红色葡萄为原料，连皮带汁一起发酵酿制而成的酒。因酒液中溶有葡萄皮的色素，故酒液呈红色，但陈酿时间越长，其颜色越浅。红葡萄酒通常在室温下饮用，20℃为最佳饮用温度，在有条件的情况下应提前开瓶，让酒与空气接触，以提高芳香度。

（1）头等舱红酒服务标准。

头等舱使用葡萄酒杯服务，提供标准：示瓶—介绍—开瓶—放酒杯—尝酒—斟酒—续酒，详见表 1-7-7。

表 1-7-7　头等舱红酒服务流程

中　文	英　文	服　务
示瓶	Show the wine bottle to passenger.	示瓶时用餐巾布托住瓶体，一手虎口卡住瓶颈，一手托瓶底。靠近旅客一侧手高。
介绍	Introduce the wine to passenger.	主动为旅客介绍酒的全称，将酒的商标（产地、公司、年限等）展示出来，请旅客过目。
开瓶	Open the bottle of the wine.	旅客认可后，回服务间开瓶。瓶盖打开后，用餐巾纸把瓶口擦拭干净，把瓶口的酒稍倒掉一点，以免有木屑浮在上面。
放酒杯	Put the wine glasses on the tray table.	将酒杯放于头等舱两座位之间的扶手台面或小桌板上，并提前放好杯垫。特别注意，拿酒杯时，应拿酒杯的下 1/3 处。
尝酒	Serve a little wine for the passenger to try the taste of the wine.	先为旅客倒一点酒请旅客品尝（如男士与女士同行，应请男士品尝，认可后再给女士斟酒），旅客认可后，为旅客斟倒。
斟酒	Pour the wine glasses.	倒酒时，瓶口不可触及杯沿，抬起瓶时慢慢转动酒瓶以免滴在桌上。葡萄酒应倒酒杯的 1/3。
续酒	Supply more wine if needed.	如旅客需要续酒，应采用示瓶的方式拿出酒瓶，当着旅客面为旅客续酒。

图 1-7-1　红酒服务

（2）经济舱红酒服务。

① Use plastic or paper cup for wine service.

② Showing the bottle is not needed when serving in the economy class.

③ Wine should be poured into one third of the glass.

二、白葡萄酒（White Wine）

白葡萄酒是以青绿色葡萄为原料，去皮后仅取葡萄的肉、汁发酵酿制而成的酒。因葡萄皮不参加发酵过程，故酒液中没有葡萄皮的色素而呈浅黄色，但陈酿时间越长，其颜色越深。

白葡萄酒需冷藏后饮用，10 ~ 12℃为最佳饮用温度。

三、香槟酒（Champagne）

香槟酒是有汽葡萄酒的典型代表。法国政府规定，只有在法国香槟地区生产的有汽葡萄酒才可称为香槟，而在其他地区或国家出产的产品只能称为有汽葡萄酒。德国是世界上有汽葡萄酒的最大生产国和消耗国，其名品有霍克（Sparkling Hock）、利富罗美（Sparkling Liebfraumilch）、莫泽尔（Sparkling Moselle）等，其出口国外的产品通常称为塞克特（Sekt）。

有汽葡萄酒含有大量的二氧化碳，所以应冷藏后饮用，其最佳饮用温度为 6℃ ~ 8℃。

Before opening the champagne, CA must be aware that the bottle is chilled enough.

—Open the wire loop.

—Hold the bottle 45 degrees.

—Do not pull the cork, but turn it firmly and the pressure in the bottle will push it out.

—To prevent the overflow of wine, CA should point the bottle top towards the galley sink area.

四、啤酒（Beer）

啤酒是以大麦为原料、啤酒花为香料经发酵酿制而成的一种含有大量二氧化碳气体的低度酒。在欧美一些国家和地区，啤酒被认为是一种饮料。啤酒具有显著的麦芽和酒花清香，口味纯正爽口，内含丰富的营养成分，所以深受人们喜爱。

外国啤酒的名品有荷兰的喜力（Heineken），德国的卢云堡（Lowenbrau）、贝克（Beck's），丹麦的嘉士伯（Carlsberg）、图波（Turborg），爱尔兰的健力士（Guinness，又称吉尼斯，其黑啤非常有名），美国的百威（Budweiser），日本的麒麟（Kirin）、札幌（Sapporo），新加坡的虎牌（Tiger），等等。

䓤啤酒适合冷藏饮用，不应加冰，其最佳饮用温度为 8 ~ 10℃。

䓤罐装啤酒应附听为旅客一并送出。

第三节　鸡尾酒

鸡尾酒是以一种或几种烈性酒如 Rum、Brandy、Whisky、Vodka 或葡萄酒未基酒与其他配料如汽水、果汁、苦精、利口酒、糖、鸡蛋等材料一起用搅拌法或摇荡调制而成的混合饮料。再加以装饰物如柠檬片、橘子皮、橄榄或樱桃等。一杯好的鸡尾酒应色、香、味、形俱佳。鸡尾酒酒味温和，酒度适中，一般在 10~20 度之间。

1. 高波（Whisky Soda）

（1）原料：威士忌 1.5 盎司①、苏打水适量。

（2）工具：高玻璃杯。

（3）饰物：橙片。

（4）制作：威士忌 1.5 盎司+冰块放入玻璃杯+适量的冰镇苏打水，饰橙片。

2. 红眼睛（Red Eye）

（1）原料：啤酒 2 盎司、番茄汁 2 盎司。

（2）工具：高玻璃杯。

（3）制作：高玻璃杯+冰镇啤酒 2 盎司+冰镇番茄汁 2 盎司。

---

① 1 盎司≈28 克。

3. 巴那西（Panache）

（1）原料：啤酒 2 盎司、七喜 2 盎司。

（2）工具：高玻璃杯。

（3）制作：高玻璃杯+冰镇啤酒 2 盎司+冰镇七喜 2 盎司。

思考与练习

Practice

一、讨论并总结 Discuss and Summarize

1. 每个小组复习并收集一个种类的酒来制作 PPT，内容包括：酒的酿造、口感、饮用习惯。每组派一名代表进行 PPT 讲解展示。

Make a powerpoint about one kind of liquor including the brewing method, taste, drinking habit by each group. One representative in the group make the presentation to classmates.

2. 请概括总结鸡尾酒 Red Eye 的基本构成。

Conclude the contents and making method of Red Eye.

二、实操技能训练 Practical Skills Training

1. 葡萄酒的拿酒姿势和斟酒技能。

Practice the holding posture and filling skills when serving the wine.

2. 制作鸡尾酒。

Make one kind of cocktail.

3. 结合服务用语模拟练习酒类服务程序。

Stimulate the alcoholic beverages serving procedures with the standard service words.

三、多选题 Multiple Choice

下列关于服务机上葡萄酒的说法正确的是：

A. 白葡萄酒乘务员需要提前进行冰镇后再发放。

B. 红葡萄酒一般保存的温度比白葡萄酒低。

C. 一般红酒需要提前开启，让其醒发，达到最佳口感。

D. 一般情况下红葡萄酒的受欢迎程度在机上服务时略高于白葡萄酒。

What is true about the wine serving on board?

A. The white wine should be cooled before serving.

B. The storage temperature of red wine is lower than white wine.

C. Red wine should be opened to proof in the air before serving to achieve the best taste.

D. The popularity of red wine serving is higher than white wine.

项目二　国际航线 CIQ 规章及单据填写

一、项目描述

国际航线和国内航线除了飞行时间、服务流程等不同之外，最大的区别在于出入境流程方面，随着国内航空公司逐渐扩展国际航线业务，航班出入境的相关规定和办理程序成为乘务员必须具备的专业知识和能力要求。

通过本章的学习与练习让同学们理解海关、边防检查、检验检疫部门的职能范围和规定，了解出境和入境手续的办理流程，能够正确填写海关单、入境单，能够引导旅客填写各种单据，帮助旅客通过出入境。

二、学习目标

（一）知识目标

1. 了解海关的职能和规定。
2. 了解边防检查的职能和规定。
3. 了解检验检疫的职能和规定。

（二）能力目标

1. 能够掌握海关单、入境单的填写规定。
2. 能够正确填写海关申报单、入境卡。
3. 能够掌握国际航班检验检疫。

（三）素养目标

1. 具备国际航线乘务员岗位要求的素养，有严谨的工作态度、较强的服务意识和良好的职业道德素养。

2. 具有良好的职业道德与契约精神，良好的与人沟通能力和团队合作精神。

3. 具有爱国、敬业、诚信、友善的精神，忠于职守，克己奉公，服务乘客，服务社会的职业精神。

单元一　中国 CIQ 规章和单据填写

第一节　海　关

图 2-1-1　中国海关关徽

海关是依据本国（或地区）的法律、行政法规行使进出口监督管理职权的国家行政机关。英语 customs 一词，最早是指商人贩运商品途中缴纳的一种地方税捐，带有“买路钱”或港口、市场“通过费”“使用费”的性质。这种地方税捐取消后，customs 一词则专指政府征收的进出口税，the Customs 是征收进出口税的政府机构，即海关，是对出入国境的一切商品和物品进行监督、检查并照章征收关税的国家机关。

中国海关负责组织推动口岸“大通关”建设、海关监管工作、进出口关税及其他税费征收管理、出入境卫生检疫和出入境动植物及其产品检验检疫、进出口商品法定检验、海关风险管理、国家进出口货物贸易等海关统计、全国打击走私综合治理工作。

一、中国海关规定

有需要向海关申报的物品走“红色通道”，没有携带向海关申报的物品走“绿色通道”。

（1）实行新的进出境旅客申报制度后，入境旅客携带有下列物品的，须填写《进出境旅客行李物品申报单》，并选择“申报通道”通关：

① 动、植物及其产品，微生物、生物制品、人体组织、血液制品；

② 居民旅客在境外获取总值超过人民币 5 000 元（含 5 000 元，下同）的自用物品；

③ 非居民旅客拟留在境内的总值超过人民币 2 000 元的物品；

④ 超过 1 500 毫升的酒精饮料，或超过 400 支的香烟，或超过 100 支的雪茄，或超过 500 克的烟丝；

⑤ 超过 20 000 元的人民币现钞，或折合超过 5 000 美元的外币现钞；

⑥ 分离运输行李，货物、货样、广告品；

⑦ 其他需要向海关申报的物品。

（2）实行新的进出境旅客申报制度后，出境旅客携带有下列物品的，须填写《进出境旅客行李物品申报单》，并选择“申报通道”通关：

① 文物、濒危动植物及其制品、生物物种资源、金银等贵重金属；

② 居民旅客携带需复带进境的单价超过人民币 5 000 元的照相机、摄像机、手提电脑等旅行自用物品；

③ 超过 20 000 元的人民币现钞，或折合超过 5 000 美元的外币现钞；

④ 货物、货样、广告品；

⑤ 其他需要向海关申报的物品。

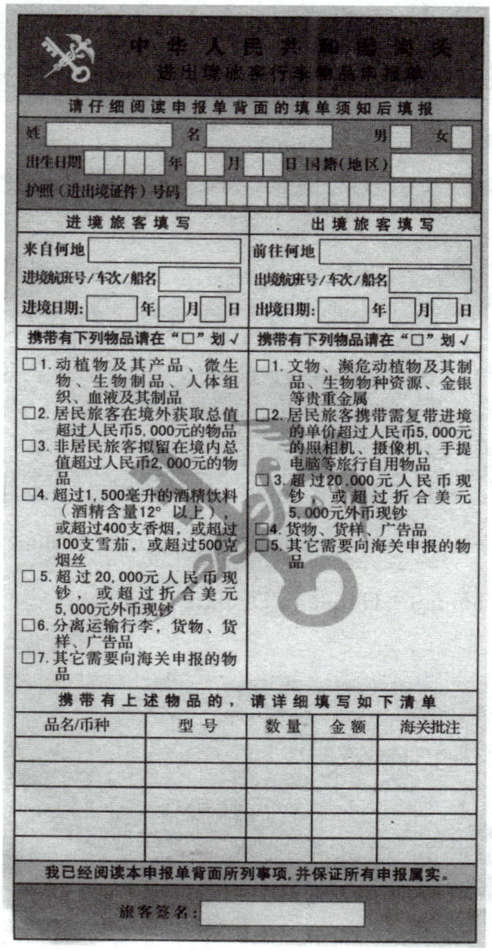
中华人民共和国海关
进出境旅客行李物品申报单

请仔细阅读申报单背面的填单须知后填报

姓　　名　　男　女

出生日期　年　月　日　国籍（地区）

护照（进出境证件）号码

进境旅客填写	出境旅客填写
来自何地	前往何地
进境航班号/车次/船名	出境航班号/车次/船名
进境日期：　年　月　日	出境日期：　年　月　日
携带有下列物品请在“□”划√	携带有下列物品请在“□”划√
□1. 动植物及其产品、微生物、生物制品、人体组织、血液及其制品	□1. 文物、濒危动植物及其制品、生物物种资源、金银等贵重金属
□2. 居民旅客在境外获取总值超过人民币5,000元的物品	□2. 居民旅客携带需复带进境的单价超过人民币5,000元的照相机、摄像机、手提电脑等旅行自用物品
□3. 非居民旅客拟留在境内总值超过人民币2,000元的物品	□3. 超过20,000元人民币现钞，或超过折合美元5,000元外币现钞
□4. 超过1,500毫升的酒精饮料（酒精含量12° 以上），或超过400支香烟，或超过100支雪茄，或超过500克烟丝	□4. 货物、货样、广告品
□5. 超过20,000元人民币现钞，或超过折合美元5,000元外币现钞	□5. 其它需要向海关申报的物品
□6. 分离运输行李，货物、货样、广告品	
□7. 其它需要向海关申报的物品	

携带有上述物品的，请详细填写如下清单

品名/币种	型号	数量	金额	海关批注

我已经阅读本申报单背面所列事项，并保证所有申报属实。

旅客签名：

图 2-1-2　中华人民共和国海关进出境旅客行李物品申报单

二、中国香港（地区）海关规定

（1）红色和绿色通道（Red and Green Channel System）。

To expedite the clearance of arriving passengers, the Department implements the "Red & Green Channel System" at all entry points. Incoming passengers are advised to choose the appropriate channels for Customs clearance with the following signs being posted:

图 2-1-3　Red Channel of Hongkong Customs

图 2-1-4　Green Channel of Hongkong Customs

① 红色通道 Red Channel（Goods to Declare Channel）。

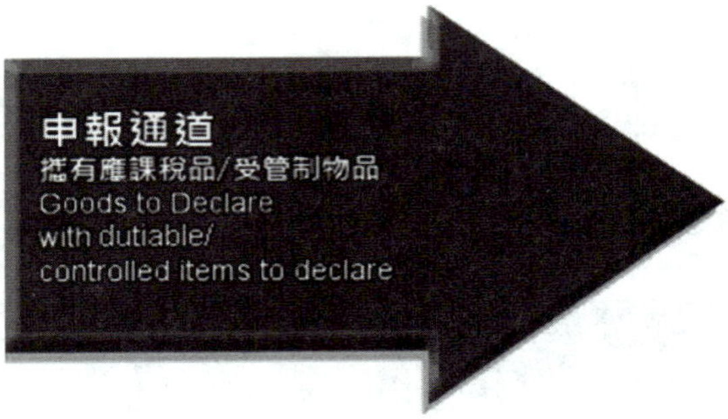

图 2-1-5　Red Channel Guide of Hongkong Customs

Passengers should proceed to this channel upon their arrival and make a declaration to the Customs officers if they carry:

• any prohibited/controlled items;

• any dutiable commodities not entitled to or exceeding their exempted quantities; and/or

• a large quantity of currency and bearer negotiable instruments ("CBNIs") (i.e. CBNIs of a total value more than HKD120,000 or the equivalent in foreign currencies).

Passengers are liable to:

• prosecution and confiscation of the prohibited/controlled items if they are unable to produce a valid licence or permit;

• duty payment on/confiscation of the dutiable commodities not entitled to or in excess of the exempted quantities; and/or

• prosecution and confiscation of the CBNIs if the declaration made contains information that is false in a material particular.

② 绿色通道 Green Channel（Nothing to Declare Channel）。

图 2-1-6　Green Channel Guide of Hongkong Customs

Passengers should enter this channel upon their arrival if they:

• do not have any dutiable goods or prohibited/controlled items;

• have dutiable goods in compliance with the exempted quantities; and/or

• are in possession of CBNIs with a total value of HKD120,000 or below (or the equivalent in foreign currencies).

Passengers entering the Green Channel are liable to:

• prosecution/penalty if they are found having undeclared/incompletely declared dutiable commodities;

• prosecution and confiscation of the prohibited/controlled items if they are found having any of them without a valid licence/permit.

• prosecution and confiscation of the CBNIs if they are found in possession of a large quantity of CBNIs without making a declaration.

They are not exempted from any Customs examination when using the Green Channel.

（2）应缴税品（Dutiable Commodities）。

• Liquor.

• Tobacco.

• Hydrocarbon Oil.

• Methyl Alçohol.

（3）饮用酒类（Alcoholic Liquor）。

A passenger aged 18 or above is allowed to bring into Hong Kong, for his own use, 1 litre of alcoholic liquor with an alcoholic strength above 30% by volume measured at a temperature of 20 ℃ exempted from duty.

If the passenger holds a Hong Kong Identity Card, he must have spent 24 hours or longer outside Hong Kong.

（4）烟草（Tobacco)。

A passenger aged 18 or above is allowed to bring into Hong Kong, for his own use, the following quantity of tobacco products exempted from duty:

• 19 cigarettes; or

• 1 cigar or 25 grams of cigars; or

• 25 grams of other manufactured tobacco.

Not for trade, business or commercial purposes

（5）海关申报。

Importation/exportation of any prohibited/controlled items into or out of the Hong Kong Special Administrative Region (HKSAR) is governed by laws.

The commonly found prohibited/controlled items are dangerous drugs, psychotropic substances, controlled chemicals, antibiotics, arms, ammunition, weapons, fireworks, strategic commodities, rough diamonds, animals, plants, endangered species, telecommunication equipment, game, meat, poultry, eggs and powdered formula.

Passengers are liable to prosecution if these items are brought into/out of HKSAR without a valid licence, permit, health certificate or written permission. These items will also be seized and confiscated.

The penalty for passengers carrying prohibited/controlled item depends on the respective legislation governing its importation and exportation.

三、日本海关规定

（1）免税限额（Duty-free/Tax-free Allowance），详见表 2-1-1。

表 2-1-1　日本免税限额

<table>
<tr><th colspan="2">Item</th><th>Allowance (for an adult)</th><th>Remarks</th></tr>
<tr><td colspan="2">Alcoholic Beverages</td><td>3 bottles</td><td>A bottle contains approximately 760cc.</td></tr>
<tr><td rowspan="4">Tobacco Products</td><td>Cigars</td><td>50 cigars</td><td rowspan="4">If a visitor brings in more than one kind of tobacco product, the total allowance is equivalent to 250 grams.
Examples of the allowance for heat-not-burn tobacco.
• IQOS: 200 pieces
• glo: 200 pieces
• Ploom TECH: 50 capsules</td></tr>
<tr><td>Cigarettes</td><td>200 cigarettes</td></tr>
<tr><td>Heat-not-burn tobacco</td><td>10 individual packages,etc</td></tr>
<tr><td>Other kinds of tobacco</td><td>250 grams</td></tr>
<tr><td colspan="2">Perfume</td><td>2 ounces</td><td>One ounce is about 28ml.</td></tr>
<tr><td colspan="2">Others</td><td>200,000 yen</td><td>The total overseas market value of all articles other than the above items must be under 200,000 yen. Any item whose overseas market value is under 10,000 yen is free of duty and/or tax and is not included in the calculation of the total overseas market value of all articles. There is no duty-free allowance for articles having a market value of more than 200,000 yen each or each set.</td></tr>
</table>

（2）禁止入境物品（Prohibited Articles）。

The following articles are prohibited from entry by law:

① Heroin, cocaine, MDMA, opium, cannabis, stimulants, psychotropic substances, and other narcotic drugs (excluding those designated by Ministry of Health, Labour and Welfare Ordinance);

② Firearms (pistols, etc.), ammunition (bullets) thereof, and pistol parts;

③ Explosives (dynamite, gunpowder, etc.);

④ Precursor materials for chemical weapons;

⑤ Counterfeit, altered, or imitation coins, paper money, bank notes, or securities, and forged credit cards;

⑥ Books, drawings, carvings, and any other article which may harm public safety or morals (obscene or immoral materials, e.g., pornography);

⑦ Child pornography; and

⑧ Articles which infringe upon intellectual property rights.

四、澳大利亚海关规定

（1）生物安全程序（Biosecurity Procedures）。

Australia has very strict biosecurity procedures at our international borders to prevent the introduction of harmful pests and diseases. Certain food items brought into Australia, even small amounts or ingredients for cooking, need to be declared.

✓	Dried herbs (including ginseng and saffron) and loose herbal teas	Food and drink	DECLARE IT
✓	Fish (excluding salmon or trout)	Food and drink	DECLARE IT
✓	Fish (salmonid species including salmon and trout)	Food and drink	DECLARE IT
✕	Food from the plane or ship	Food and drink	DON'T BRING
?	Honey products	Food and drink	DECLARE IT
✓	Human breast milk	Food and drink	DECLARE IT

图 2-1-7　Biosecurity Declaration of Australia Customs

（2）免税限额（Duty free items）。

① General Goods: adults — AUD 900, kids — AUD 450.

② Alcohol — 2.25 litres.

③ Tobacco — 25 cigarettes or 25g tobacco.

There may be airline rules about cabin or hold baggage or aviation safety laws that mean you can't take certain items in the cabin or on the plane.

（3）植物、花朵和种子（Plants, flowers and seeds）。

✕	Live plants	Plants, flowers and seeds	DON'T BRING
?	Seeds	Plants, flowers and seeds	DECLARE IT

图 2-1-8　Plants and Seeds Declaration of Australia Customs

（4）武器（Weapons）。

There may be airline rules about cabin or hold baggage or aviation safety laws that mean you can't take certain items in the cabin or on the plane.

✕	Automatic knives	Weapons	DON'T BRING
✕	Balisong/Butterfly knives	Weapons	DON'T BRING
✕	Blowguns	Weapons	DON'T BRING
✕	Concealed blades	Weapons	DON'T BRING
✕	Daggers	Weapons	DON'T BRING
✕	Electric shock devices	Weapons	DON'T BRING
✕	Extendable batons	Weapons	DON'T BRING

图 2-1-9　Weapon Declaration

五、美国海关规定

（1）非居民（Non Residents）。

• Tobacco products : 200 cigarettes and 100 cigars.

• 1L of alcohol for persons of 21 years or older.

• Other goods for personal use.

• USD 100 worth of dutiable items as a gift.

• Non-residents are allowed up to $100 worth of merchandise. To claim this exemption, you must remain in the United States for at least 72 hours, and the gifts must accompany you.

This $100 gift exemption can be claimed only once every six months. You may include 100 cigars within the gift exemption, but alcoholic beverages may not be included. Family members may not group their gift exemptions. If you've used your gift exemption and then return to the United States before the six-month period has ended, you may still bring in up to $200 worth of merchandise free of duty for your personal. Any of the following may be included in this $200 exemption:

— 50 cigarettes.

— 100 cigars (non-Cuban).

— 150 ml of alcoholic beverages.

— 150 ml of perfume containing alcohol, or equivalent amounts of each.

If you exceed any of these limitations, however, or if the total value of all dutiable articles exceeds $200, no exemption can be applied.

（2）居民（Residents）。

• Exemption of USD 200 worth of dutiable items:

For residents that travelled abroad more than once in a 30-day period or who have been out of the country for at least 48 hours. If the worth of the items brought in exceeds the above USD200 then the whole amount is dutiable. You may include with the $200 exemption your choice of the following:

— 50 cigarettes and

— 10 cigars and

— 150 ml (5 fl. oz.) of alcoholic beverages or

— 150 ml (5 fl. oz.) of perfume containing alcohol.

（3）禁止入境货物（Prohibited Goods）。

Applicable for residents of U.S.A and non-resident:

• Eat or any products thereof (dried, canned etc.).

• Narcotics and some medication containing prohibited substances.

• Absinthe (unless thujone free).

• Plants, seeds, vegetables, fruits.

• Soil, livestock or animal pests.

• Biological (bacteria cultures, fungi specimens, viruses and others for research and etc. permissible only with APHIS permit).

• Unprepared fish and fish eggs.

• Imports from embargoed countries (Iran, Cuba, Myanmar, Sudan) and leather souvenirs imported from Haiti (drums).

• Endangered wildlife species and products thereof (for example clothing and accessories)

• Cultural artefacts from Byzantine period, Pre-Columbian period, Khmer sculptures (unless with permission).

• Dog and cat fur.

• Items infringing trade and copyright regulations.

• Fully automatic weapons and semi-automatic weapons (see the restricted section).

• Pornography.

• Articles infringing copyrights.

• Traitorous material and material igniting agitation.

• Hazardous articles like fireworks, uncertified toys, health hazardous substances.

第二节　边防检查

边防检查涉及的常见词组详见表 2-1-2。

表 2-1-2　边防检查常见词组

中　文	英　文
中国边检	China Immigration Inspection
护照	passport
港澳通行证	exit & entry permit for travelling to and from Hong Kong and Macao
台湾通行证	exit & entry permit for travelling to and from Taiwan
签证	visa

中国出入境卡（仅供外国人使用），中国国籍居民从中国大陆到香港、澳门、台湾不需填写出入境卡。

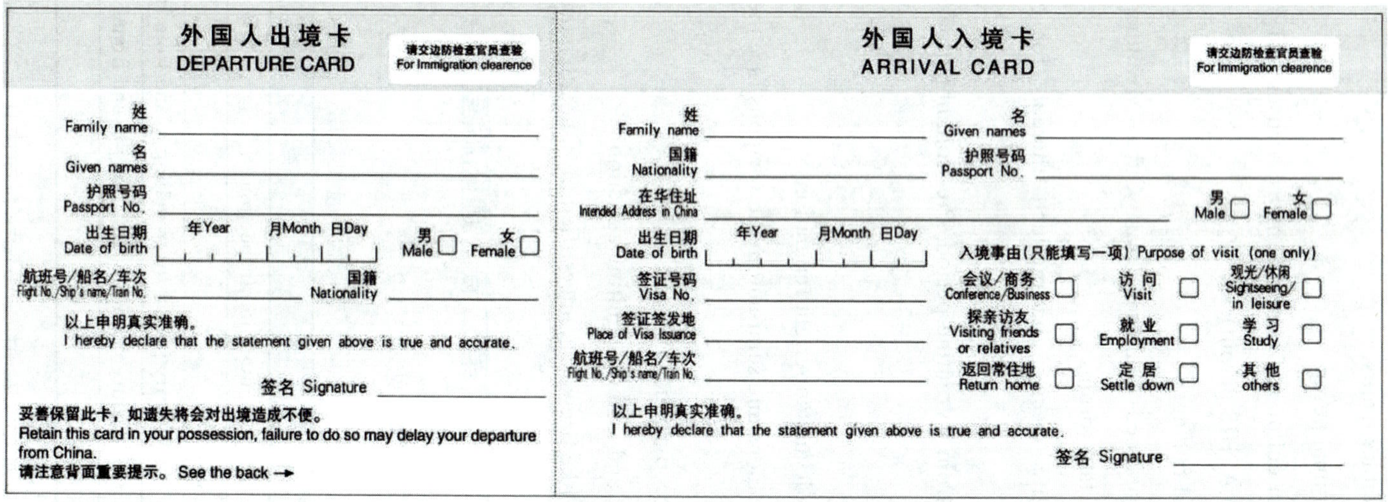

图 2-1-10　中国出入境卡

第三节 检验检疫

出入境检验是为国家进行出入境检验检疫工作的部门。职责是对出入境的货物、人员、交通工具、集装箱、行李邮包携带物等进行包括卫生检疫、动植物检疫、商品检验等的检查，以保障人员、动植物安全卫生和商品的质量。

负责实施出入境卫生检疫、传染病监测和卫生监督，负责口岸传染病的预防与控制工作，负责出入境人员的预防接种和传染病监测体检的管理工作。

2018 年 4 月 14 日起，中国国家出入境检验检疫管理职责和队伍统一划入海关总署。原出入境检验检疫局和直属单位统一以海关名义对外开展工作，一线旅检、查验和窗口岗位实现统一上岗、统一着海关制服、统一佩戴关衔、统一使用海关标识。中国海关增加卫生检疫、动植物检疫、商品检验、进出口食品安全监管等职责，通过建立信息集聚、优化高效、协调统一的风险防控体系，推行全链条式管理，强化智能监管、精准监管。从而优化作业流程，减少非必要的作业环节和手续，从而降低通关成本，提升通关效率。

第四节 CIQ 相关服务

（1）乘务员应掌握各国 CIQ 规定。

（2）国际航线发放 CIQ 表格并协助旅客填写。

（3）两舱地面发完餐谱后，用托盘发放入境卡。如地面未发送，可在一餐后补送，或根据旅客需求随时提供。

图 2-1-11 乘务员为旅客提供入境卡

单元二 外国 CIQ 单据填写

第一节 韩 国

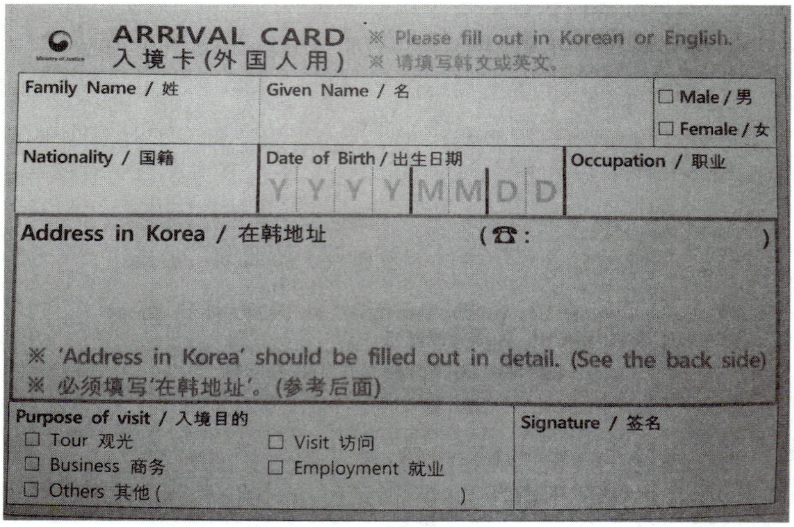

ARRIVAL CARD
入境卡(外国人用)
※ Please fill out in Korean or English.
※ 请填写韩文或英文。

Family Name / 姓
Given Name / 名
□ Male / 男
□ Female / 女
Nationality / 国籍
Date of Birth / 出生日期
Y Y Y Y M M D D
Occupation / 职业
Address in Korea / 在韩地址 (☎:)
※ 'Address in Korea' should be filled out in detail. (See the back side)
※ 必须填写'在韩地址'。(参考后面)
Purpose of visit / 入境目的
□ Tour 观光
□ Visit 访问
□ Business 商务
□ Employment 就业
□ Others 其他( )
Signature / 签名

图 2-2-1 韩国入境卡正面

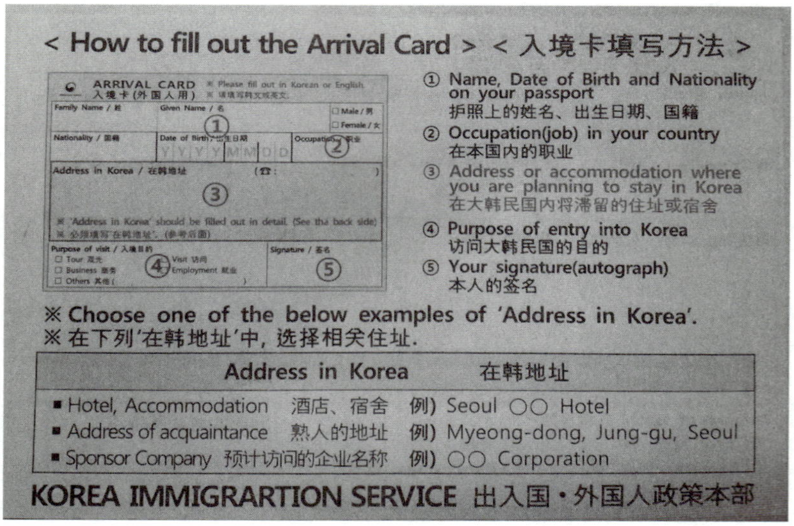

< How to fill out the Arrival Card > < 入境卡填写方法 >

① Name, Date of Birth and Nationality on your passport
护照上的姓名、出生日期、国籍
② Occupation(job) in your country
在本国内的职业
③ Address or accommodation where you are planning to stay in Korea
在大韩民国内将滞留的住址或宿舍
④ Purpose of entry into Korea
访问大韩民国的目的
⑤ Your signature(autograph)
本人的签名

※ Choose one of the below examples of 'Address in Korea'.
※ 在下列'在韩地址'中，选择相关住址.

Address in Korea	在韩地址	
▪ Hotel, Accommodation	酒店、宿舍	例) Seoul ○○ Hotel
▪ Address of acquaintance	熟人的地址	例) Myeong-dong, Jung-gu, Seoul
▪ Sponsor Company	预计访问的企业名称	例) ○○ Corporation

KOREA IMMIGRARTION SERVICE 出入国·外国人政策本部

图 2-2-2 韩国入境卡背面

游客携带物品申报单

- 所有入境人员均需填写并提交此申报单，大韩民国海关官员需要时，可随时检查旅客的行李物品。
- 以家庭为单位入境时，家庭一员代表填写即可。
- 填写前，请务必阅读申报单背面的填写须知。

姓　　名			
出生日期		护照号码	
职　　业		停留期限	日
旅行目的	□旅游　□商务　□探亲访友　□公务　□其他		
航 班 号		同行家属	人
来韩前所访国家(共　　国) 1.　　　　2.　　　　3.			
韩国地址			
联系电话（手机）	☎　　　　（　　　　）		

海关申报事项

-请在下列问题后□内划"√"。-

	是	否
1. 是否从国外(包括国内外免税店)获取(包括购买、捐赠、赠送)超出免税范围的物品(参照背面1) [总额：约　　　　] ※自行申报超过免税范围的物品时，减免30%关税(不超过15万韩币)。	□	□
2. 是否携带需要享受特殊优惠关税的FTA缔约国产品	□	□
3. 是否携带超过1万美金以上的支付工具(韩币、美金等法定货币、银行支票、旅行支票及其他有价证券等) [总额：约　　　　]	□	□
4. 是否携带韩国违禁物品与受限物品(枪支、炮弹、刀剑、毒品以及危害国家安全和社会稳定的物品)(参照背面2)	□	□
5. 是否携带动植物、肉类加工品等需要检疫的物品；是否前往过畜禽传染病发生国家的畜禽农场 ※前往畜禽农场者，需向韩国检疫本部申报	□	□
6. 是否携带销售品、公司货物(样品等)、他人委托携带品、寄存或暂准进出口货物	□	□

我保证以上所填申报内容属实无误。

年　　　月　　　日

申报人：　　　　　　　（签名）

图 2-2-3　韩国海关申报单正面

[申报物品填写栏]

▶烟·酒·香水（若超过免税范围，则应填写所有携带物品数量）

酒	（　　）瓶，共（　　）升，金额（　　）美金		
烟	（　　）盒(以20根为准)	香水	（　　）毫升

▶其他超过免税范围(600美金)的物品

品　名	数(重)量	金　额

1. 携带物品免税范围

▶烟·酒·香水

酒	香水	烟
1瓶 (不超过1升，且不超过400美金)	60毫升	200根

未满19周岁旅客所携带的烟，酒等物品，不属于免税范围。

▶其他物品

不超过600美金

(限本人使用，礼品，随身物品)

* 农林畜产品，中草药等不超过10万韩元,每种物品的数量与重量均有所限制。

2. 违禁物品与受限物品

- 枪支，炮弹，刀剑等武器与仿真武器，炸弹，雷管，火药，放射性物质，窃听装置等
- 冰毒、鸦片、海洛因、大麻等毒品与违禁医药品
- 危害国家安全，破坏社会稳定，泄露政府机密的物品
- 损害知识产权的冒牌产品，假钞，伪造有价证券等
- 熊胆，麝香，鹿茸，鳄鱼皮等濒危野生动植物与相关产品

3. 需检疫物品

- 活体动物(宠物等)，水产动物(鱼类)，鲜肉，肉脯，火腿肠，午餐肉，奶酪等肉类加工品
- 土壤，芒果，核桃，山参，松茸菌，橙子，樱桃等鲜果，坚果以及蔬菜等

※ 填写须知

- 姓名应填写护照上的韩文名或英文名。
- 若发现未申报，虚假申报或代理携带的，根据大韩民国《关税法》将判处五年以下有期徒刑或给予拘留，征收附加税（纳税额的40%,两年内超过2次的,征收60%），通告处分，没收等处罚。
- 根据FTA协议规定，凡符合一定要求的物品，均可享受特殊优惠关税，但需要事后申请特殊关税的，则应当进行一般进口申报。
- 若有其他疑问，请咨询海关官员或致电 ☎125。

图 2-2-4　韩国海关申报单反面

第二节 新加坡

表 2-2-1 常见中英对照 1

Full name as it appears in passport/travel document (BLOCK LETTERS)	旅行证件姓名（大写）
Passport number	护照号码
Place of residence city	居住地城市
State	州
Country	国家
Flight No. /Vessel name/Vehicle No.	交通工具号码
Address in Singapore	新加坡住址
Postal code	邮政编码
Contact number	联系号码
Country of birth	出生地国家
Date of birth	出生日期
Length of stay	逗留时长
Nationality	国籍
Last city/port of embarkation before Singapore	离港城市
Next city/port of disembarkation after Singapore	前往城市
Signature	签名

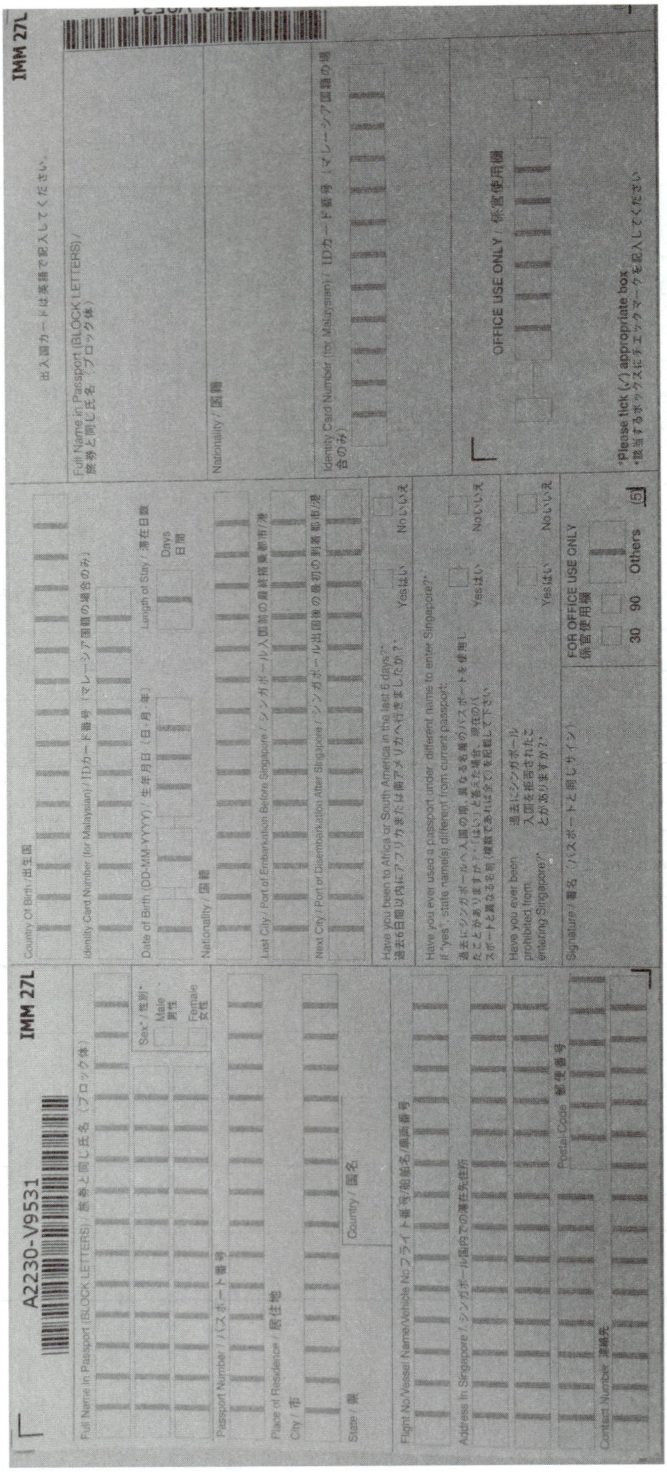
IMM 27L

A2230-V9531

IMM 27L

Full Name in Passport (BLOCK LETTERS) / 旅券と同じ氏名（ブロック体）

Sex* / 性別* Male 男性 Female 女性

Passport Number / パスポート番号

Place of Residence / 居住地

City / 市

State / 県

Country / 国名

Flight No/Vessel Name/Vehicle No フライト番号/船舶名/車両番号

Address In Singapore / シンガポール国内での滞在先住所

Postal Code 郵便番号

Contact Number 連絡先

Country Of Birth / 出生国

Identity Card Number (for Malaysian) / IDカード番号（マレーシア国籍の場合のみ）

Date of Birth (DD-MM-YYYY) / 生年月日（日・月・年）

Length of Stay / 滞在日数 Days 日間

Nationality / 国籍

Last City / Port of Embarkation Before Singapore / シンガポール入国前の最終積乗都市/港

Next City / Port of Disembarkation After Singapore / シンガポール出国後の最初の到着都市/港

Have you been to Africa or South America in the last 6 days?* 過去6日間以内にアフリカまたは南アメリカへ行きましたか？* Yes はい No いいえ

Have you ever used a passport under different name to enter Singapore?* If "yes", state name(s) different from current passport. Yes はい No いいえ

Have you ever been prohibited from entering Singapore?* 過去にシンガポール入国を拒否されたことがありますか？* Yes はい No いいえ

Signature / 署名（パスポートと同じサイン）

FOR OFFICE USE ONLY 係官使用欄 30 90 Others

IMM 27L

出入国カードは英語で記入してください。

Full Name in Passport (BLOCK LETTERS) / 旅券と同じ氏名（ブロック体）

Nationality / 国籍

Identity Card Number (for Malaysian) / IDカード番号（マレーシア国籍の場合のみ）

OFFICE USE ONLY / 係官使用欄

*Please tick (✓) appropriate box

*該当するボックスにチェックマークを記入してください

图 2-2-5 新加坡入境卡

第三节　尼泊尔

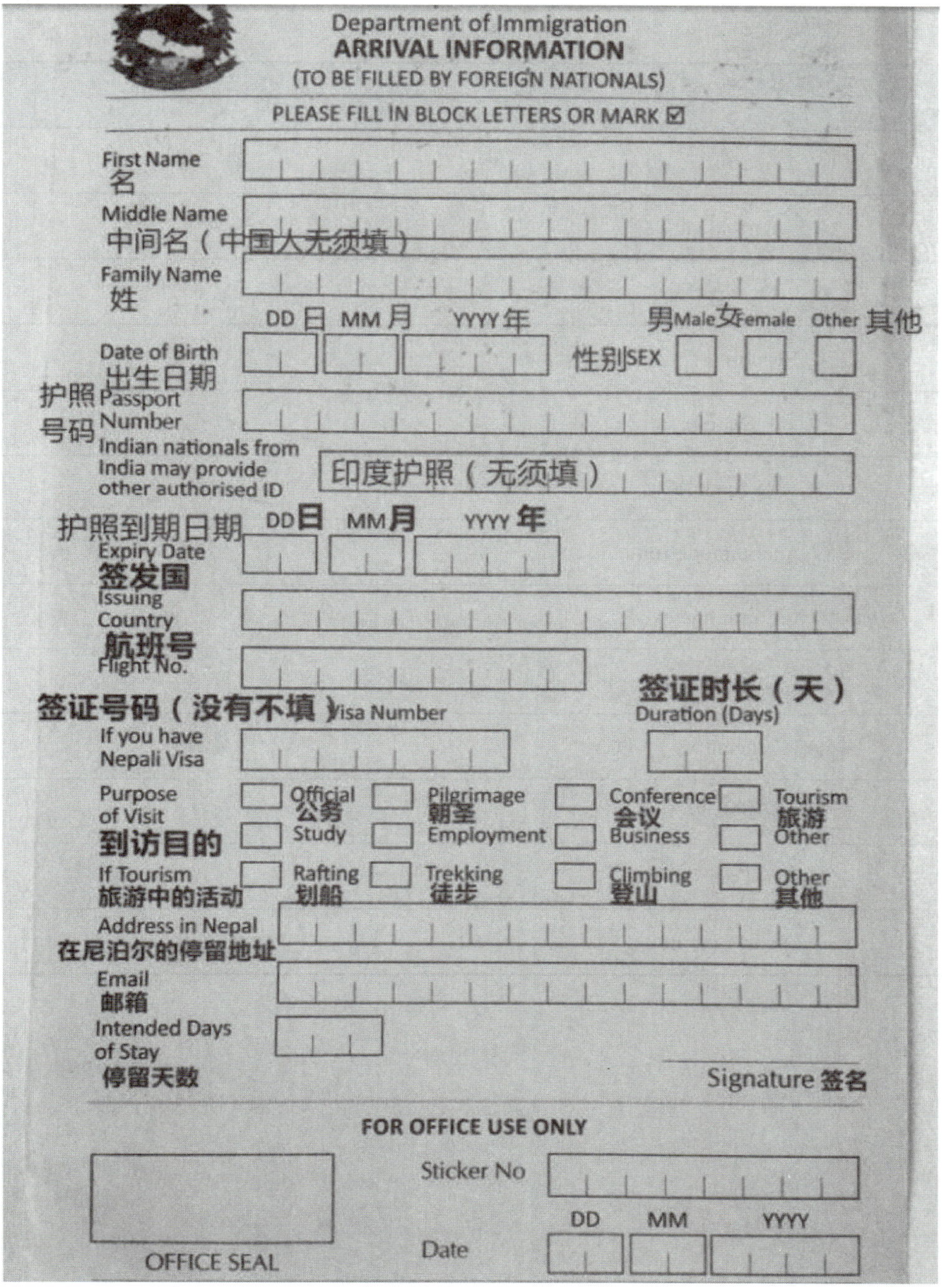

Department of Immigration
ARRIVAL INFORMATION
(TO BE FILLED BY FOREIGN NATIONALS)
PLEASE FILL IN BLOCK LETTERS OR MARK ☑

First Name 名
Middle Name 中间名（中国人无须填）
Family Name 姓
DD 日 MM 月 YYYY 年　男Male 女Female Other 其他
Date of Birth 出生日期　性别SEX
护照号码 Passport Number
Indian nationals from India may provide other authorised ID　印度护照（无须填）
护照到期日期 DD 日 MM 月 YYYY 年
Expiry Date
签发国 Issuing Country
航班号 Flight No.
签证号码（没有不填）Visa Number If you have Nepali Visa
签证时长（天）Duration (Days)
Purpose of Visit 到访目的
Official 公务　Pilgrimage 朝圣　Conference 会议　Tourism 旅游
Study　Employment　Business　Other
If Tourism 旅游中的活动
Rafting 划船　Trekking 徒步　Climbing 登山　Other 其他
Address in Nepal 在尼泊尔的停留地址
Email 邮箱
Intended Days of Stay 停留天数
Signature 签名

FOR OFFICE USE ONLY
Sticker No
DD　MM　YYYY
Date
OFFICE SEAL

图 2-2-6　尼泊尔入境卡

第四节 泰 国

表 2-2-2 常见中英对照 2

英 文	中 文
Departure card	离境卡
Arrival card	入境卡
Occupation	职业
Purpose of visit	到访目的
Charter	包机
Schedule	班机
Accommodation	住宿
Youth hostel	青年旅舍
Guest house	民宅
Incentive	奖励
Medical & Wellness	医疗
Transit	过境
Yearly income	年收入

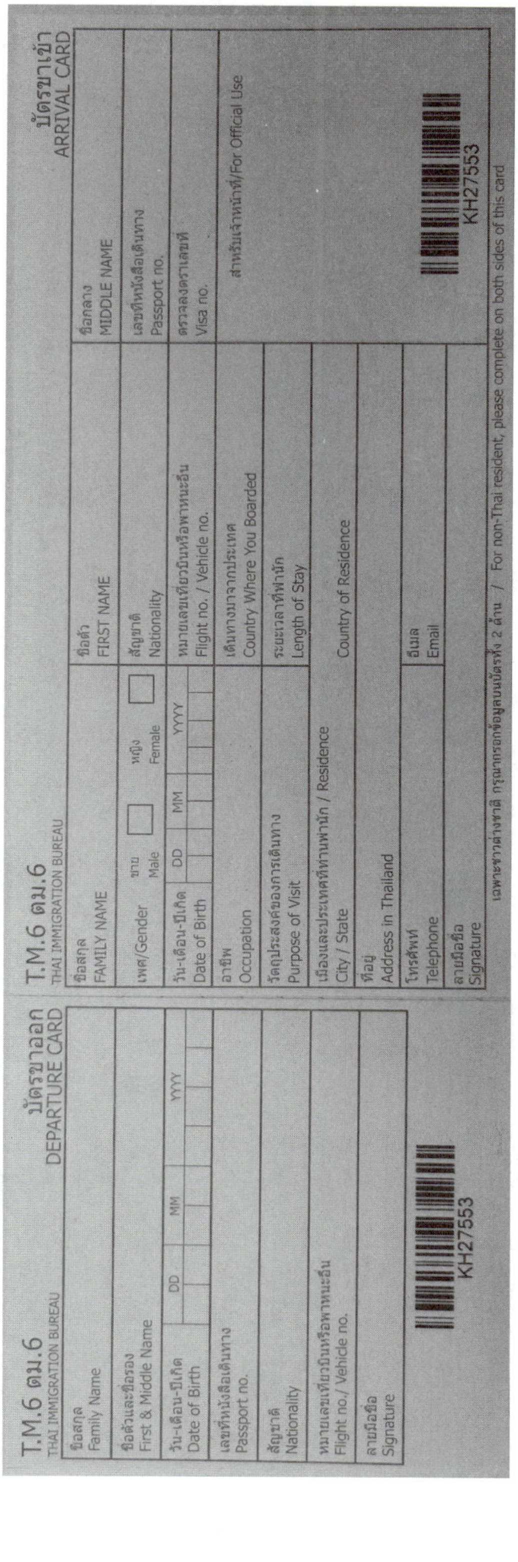

图 2-2-7　泰国入境卡及出境卡正面

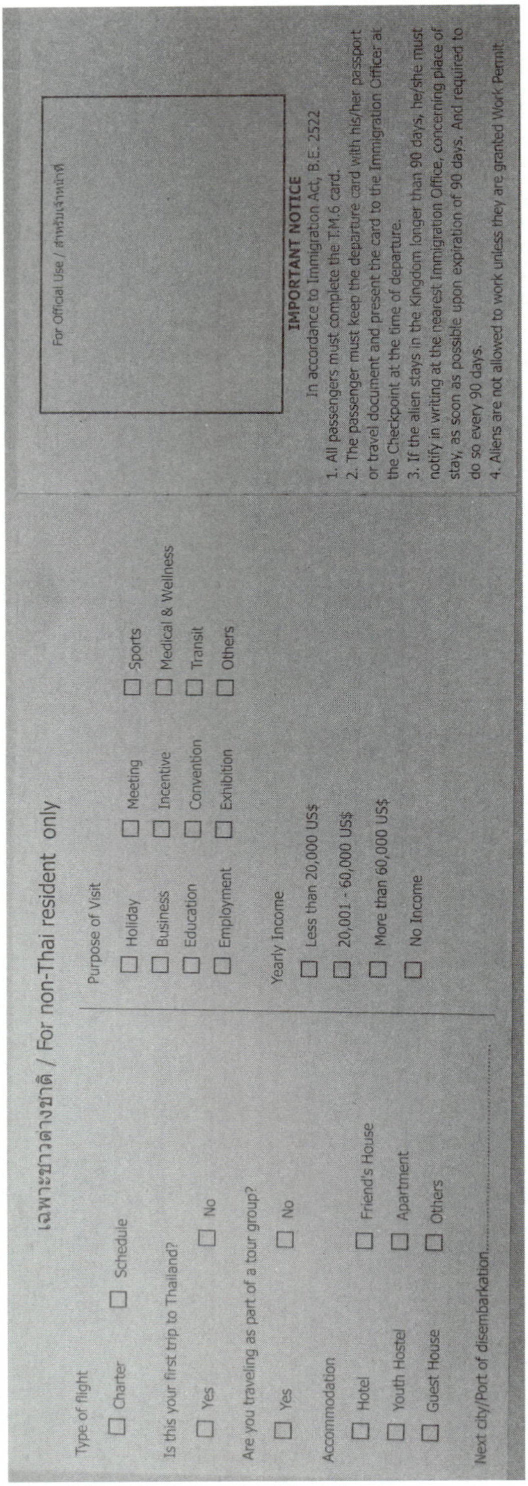
เฉพาะชาวต่างชาติ / For non-Thai resident only

Type of flight
☐ Charter ☐ Schedule

Is this your first trip to Thailand?
☐ Yes ☐ No

Are you traveling as part of a tour group?
☐ Yes ☐ No

Accommodation
☐ Hotel ☐ Friend's House
☐ Youth Hostel ☐ Apartment
☐ Guest House ☐ Others

Next city/Port of disembarkation.......................

Purpose of Visit
☐ Holiday ☐ Meeting ☐ Sports
☐ Business ☐ Incentive ☐ Medical & Wellness
☐ Education ☐ Convention ☐ Transit
☐ Employment ☐ Exhibition ☐ Others

Yearly Income
☐ Less than 20,000 US$
☐ 20,001 - 60,000 US$
☐ More than 60,000 US$
☐ No Income

For Official Use / สำหรับเจ้าหน้าที่

IMPORTANT NOTICE

In accordance to Immigration Act, B.E. 2522

1. All passengers must complete the T.M.6 card.
2. The passenger must keep the departure card with his/her passport or travel document and present the card to the Immigration Officer at the Checkpoint at the time of departure.
3. If the alien stays in the Kingdom longer than 90 days, he/she must notify in writing at the nearest Immigration Office, concerning place of stay, as soon as possible upon expiration of 90 days. And required to do so every 90 days.
4. Aliens are not allowed to work unless they are granted Work Permit.

图 2-2-8　泰国人境卡及出境卡背面

ตม.88

TM.88

Photograph

4 x 6 cm.

APPLICATION FOR VISA ON ARRIVAL

Miss.

Mr.

Mrs...

Family name　　First name　　Middle name　　(in block letters)

Nationality..............................Passport or travelling document No..............................

Date and place of issue..............................Date of birth..............................

Expiry date..............................Flight No..............................

Occupation..

Permanent address..

Address in Thailand..

Name and address of person (s) of reference in Thailand

....

....

If accompanied by minor children travelling on the same passport, please give names, dates and places of birth

....

....

....

....

....

Signature..............................

Date..............................

FOR OFFICIAL USE ONLY

Visa No. ....Date of Issue..............................

Fees..

Signature..............................

Immigration Officer

Date..............................

NOTICE

VISA FEE IS 1,000 BAHT PER PERSON

THAI CURRENCY ONLY/NON - REFUNDABLE

(โรงพิมพ์ตำรวจ พ.ศ. ๒๕๔๕)

图 2-2-9　泰国落地签申请表

第五节　日　本

日本入境卡详见图 2-2-10。

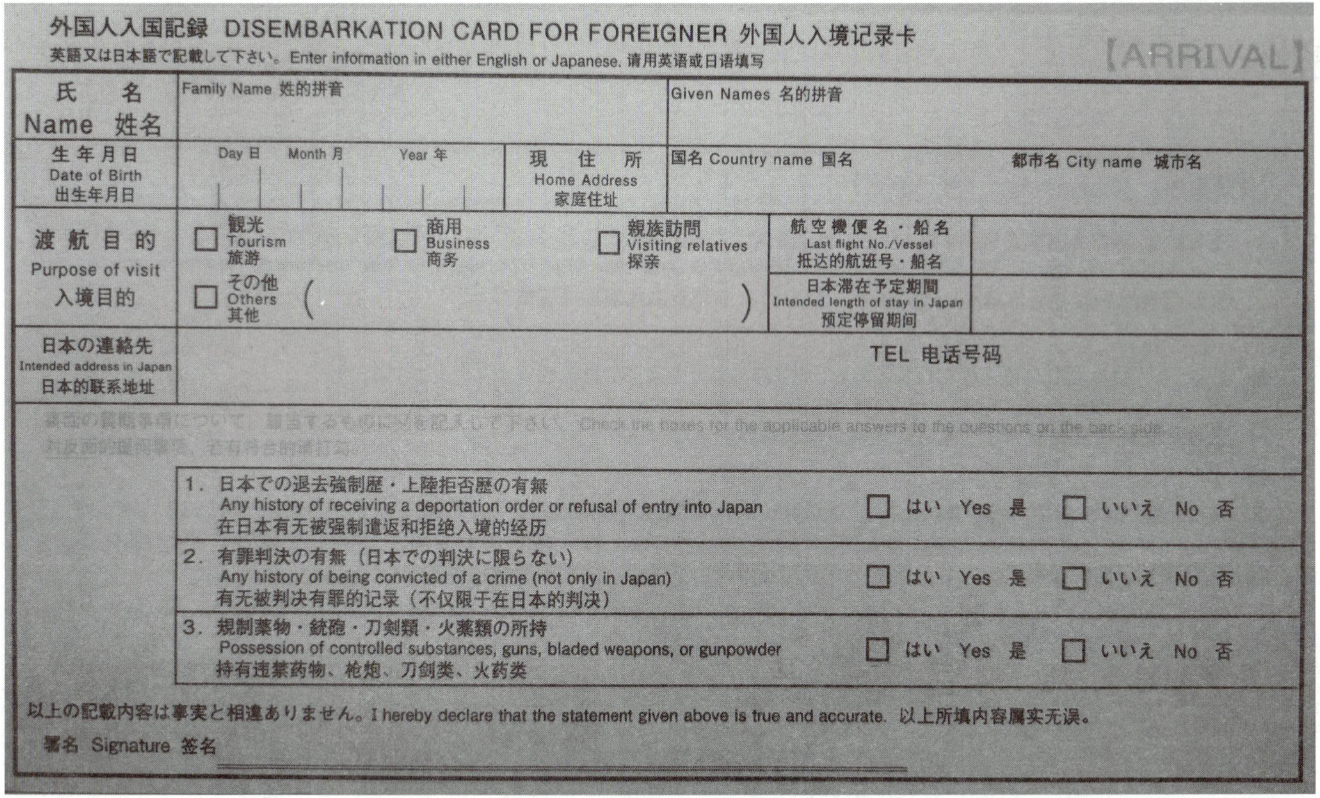

外国人入国記録 DISEMBARKATION CARD FOR FOREIGNER 外国人入境记录卡 【ARRIVAL】

英語又は日本語で記載して下さい。Enter information in either English or Japanese. 请用英语或日语填写

氏 名 Name 姓名	Family Name 姓的拼音		Given Names 名的拼音	
生年月日 Date of Birth 出生年月日	Day 日 Month 月 Year 年	現 住 所 Home Address 家庭住址	国名 Country name 国名	都市名 City name 城市名
渡航目的 Purpose of visit 入境目的	□ 観光 Tourism 旅游 □ 商用 Business 商务 □ 親族訪問 Visiting relatives 探亲 □ その他 Others 其他 (　　　)		航空機便名・船名 Last flight No./Vessel 抵达的航班号・船名 日本滞在予定期間 Intended length of stay in Japan 预定停留期间	
日本の連絡先 Intended address in Japan 日本的联系地址			TEL 电话号码	

裏面の質問事項について、該当するものに☑を記入して下さい。Check the boxes for the applicable answers to the questions on the back side. 对反面的提问事项，在有符合的请打勾。

1. 日本での退去強制歴・上陸拒否歴の有無 Any history of receiving a deportation order or refusal of entry into Japan 在日本有无被强制遣返和拒绝入境的经历	□ はい Yes 是	□ いいえ No 否
2. 有罪判決の有無（日本での判決に限らない） Any history of being convicted of a crime (not only in Japan) 有无被判决有罪的记录（不仅限于在日本的判决）	□ はい Yes 是	□ いいえ No 否
3. 規制薬物・銃砲・刀剣類・火薬類の所持 Possession of controlled substances, guns, bladed weapons, or gunpowder 持有违禁药物、枪炮、刀剑类、火药类	□ はい Yes 是	□ いいえ No 否

以上の記載内容は事実と相違ありません。I hereby declare that the statement given above is true and accurate. 以上所填内容属实无误。

署名 Signature 签名

图 2-2-10　日本入境卡

（A面）

日本海关

海关格式C第5360-D号

携带品 分离运输行李 申报单

请在下边及背面填写后，向海关职员提交。
如有同行家属，只需填写一张申报单。

航班号（船名）		出发地	
入境日期	年　月　日		
姓名	拼音		
日本的地址（逗留地）	电话　（　）		
国籍		职业	
出生日期	年　月　日		
护照号码			
同行家属	满20周岁　个人	满6周岁至未满20周岁　个人	未满6周岁　个人

※　以下有关事项，请在 □ 中划“✓”。

1．您是否有下述物品？（包含手提或寄放行李及分离运输行李等）　是　否

① 禁止或限制携入日本的物品（例如、麻药、枪支、爆炸物）（参看B面的第1及第2）　□　□

② 金条、金制品　□　□

③ 超过免税范围（参照B面的第3）的购买品、土产品、礼品等　□　□

④ 商业货物、商业样品　□　□

⑤ 由别人委托的携带物品　□　□

*携带有①-⑤项下物品的，请在B面清单里详细填写入境时携带的物品。

2．您是否有超过相当１００万日元的现钞、有价证券或超过1公斤的贵金属等？　是 □　否 □

*选择「是」的旅客还需要填写「支付手段等输出·输入申报书」提交给海关。

3．分离运输行李　入境携带物品以外，是否有邮寄物品等分离运输的物品（包括搬家物品）？

□ 是（　　个）　□ 否

*选择「是」的，请在B面的清单里填写入境时携带的物品，向海关提交两张申报单，接受海关检查验证。（限入境以后六个月以内的进口货）
确认后的申报单在分离运输行李通关时需要。

《注意事项》

例如在国外或出入日本时，于免税店购买的物品或受人委带的物品等要携带出入日本，及分离运输的物品依据法令规定都须向海关申报，有必要时须接受检查。另外，有未申报或虚伪申报等非法行为时，可能会受处罚。敬请注意。

我保证所有申报属实。

申报人签名

图 2-2-11　日本海关申报单正面

（B面）

※ 请把入境时携带的物品填入下面的表（A面的第1和第3的提问都选择「否」的旅客不需要填入。）

（注意）其他物品只限自用的物品，总额不超过1万日元的物品（据境外市价）不需填入。

除此以外，分离运输的物品不需填入。

酒类			瓶	*海关记入
烟草	香烟		支	
	加热式		盒	
	雪茄		支	
	其他		克	
香水			盎司	

其他物品的品名	数量	价格

*海关记入 日元

1．禁止携入日本主要的物品

① 麻药、向精神药、大麻、鸦片、兴奋剂、摇头丸（MDMA）、指定的药物等
② 手枪等枪支、这些枪支的弹药及零件
③ 爆炸物、火药类、化学兵器的原材料及痈疽细菌等的病原体等
④ 货币、纸币、有价证券及信用卡等的伪造物品等
⑤ 黄色杂志・激光视盘等(DVD)、以及儿童色情物品等
⑥ 假冒名牌商品、盗版等侵害知识产权的物品

2．限制携入日本主要的物品

① 猎枪、气枪、以及日本刀等的刀剑类
② 根据华盛顿条约限制进口的动植物及其制品（鳄鱼、蛇、龟、象牙、麝香及仙人掌等）
③ 有必要事前检疫的动植物、肉类产品（包括香肠、牛肉干等）、蔬菜、水果及大米等
* 务必先接受动植物检疫。

3．免税范围（每人，乘务员除外）

・酒类:3瓶（按：760ml折合）
・香烟:400支（不分国内外制品）
* 未满20周岁的人不适用酒类和烟草的免税范围。
・境外市价的总额不超过20万日元的物品（只限入境者自用的物品。）
* 境外市价是在外国通常的零售价格（购买价格）。
* 价格20万日元以上的单件物品，价格全部上税。
* 未满6周岁的幼儿，除了玩具等幼儿本人使用的物品以外，不适用免税范围。

感谢您填写携带品・分离运输行李的申报单。根据法令，入境日本的所有的旅客都需要填写申报单并提交海关。感谢您继续配合海关的检查。

图 2-2-12　日本海关申报单背面

第六节　英　国

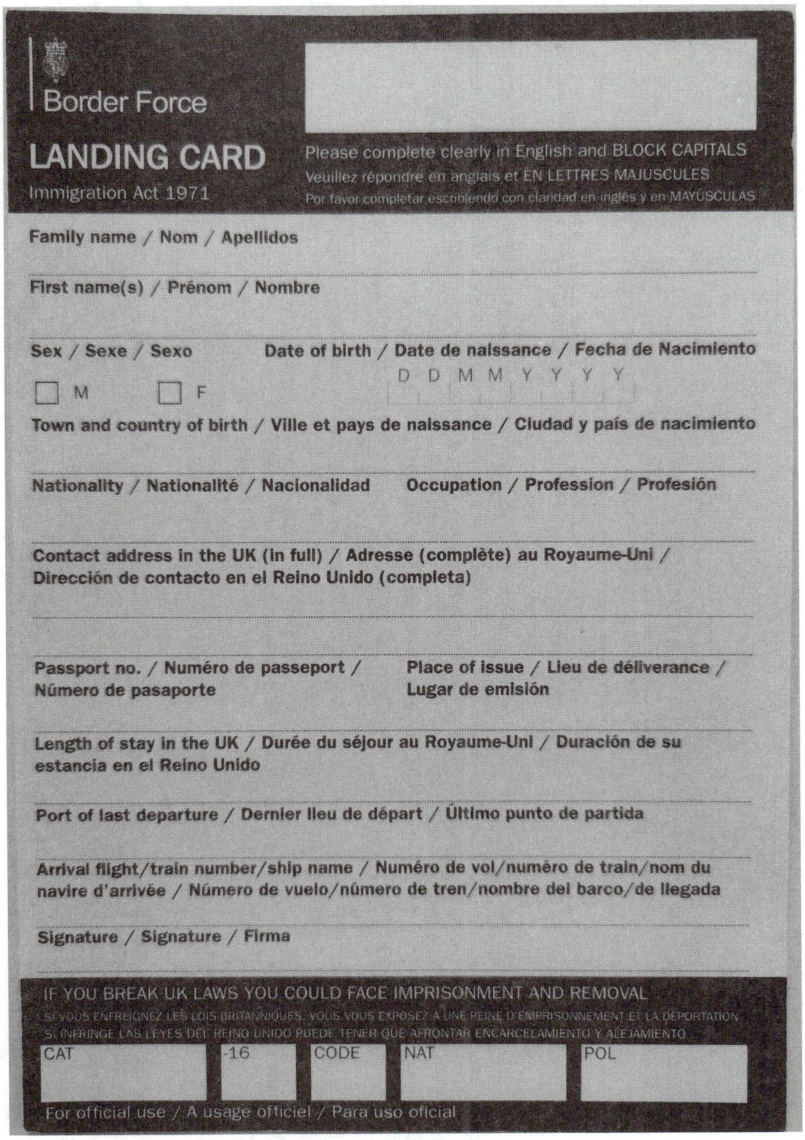
Border Force

LANDING CARD

Immigration Act 1971

Please complete clearly in English and BLOCK CAPITALS
Veuillez répondre en anglais et EN LETTRES MAJUSCULES
Por favor completar escribiendo con claridad en inglés y en MAYÚSCULAS

Family name / Nom / Apellidos

First name(s) / Prénom / Nombre

Sex / Sexe / Sexo　□ M　□ F

Date of birth / Date de naissance / Fecha de Nacimiento　D D M M Y Y Y Y

Town and country of birth / Ville et pays de naissance / Ciudad y país de nacimiento

Nationality / Nationalité / Nacionalidad

Occupation / Profession / Profesión

Contact address in the UK (in full) / Adresse (complète) au Royaume-Uni / Dirección de contacto en el Reino Unido (completa)

Passport no. / Numéro de passeport / Número de pasaporte

Place of issue / Lieu de délivrance / Lugar de emisión

Length of stay in the UK / Durée du séjour au Royaume-Uni / Duración de su estancia en el Reino Unido

Port of last departure / Dernier lieu de départ / Último punto de partida

Arrival flight/train number/ship name / Numéro de vol/numéro de train/nom du navire d'arrivée / Número de vuelo/número de tren/nombre del barco/de llegada

Signature / Signature / Firma

IF YOU BREAK UK LAWS YOU COULD FACE IMPRISONMENT AND REMOVAL
SI VOUS ENFREIGNEZ LES LOIS BRITANNIQUES, VOUS VOUS EXPOSEZ À UNE PEINE D'EMPRISONNEMENT ET LA DÉPORTATION
SI INFRINGE LAS LEYES DEL REINO UNIDO PUEDE TENER QUE AFRONTAR ENCARCELAMIENTO Y ALEJAMIENTO

CAT	-16	CODE	NAT	POL

For official use / A usage officiel / Para uso oficial

图 2-2-13　英国入境卡

第七节　澳大利亚

澳大利亚入境卡正反面详见图 2-2-14 和 2-2-15，澳大利亚出境卡详见图 2-2-16。

Incoming passenger card • Australia

PLEASE COMPLETE IN ENGLISH WITH A BLUE OR BLACK PEN

- Family/surname
- Given names
- Passport number
- Flight number or name of ship
- Intended address in Australia

State

- Do you intend to live in Australia for the next 12 months? Yes No
- If you are **NOT an Australian citizen**:
  - Do you have tuberculosis? Yes No
  - Do you have any criminal conviction/s? Yes No

YOU MUST ANSWER EVERY QUESTION – IF UNSURE, Yes ✕

Are you bringing into Australia:

1. Goods that may be prohibited or subject to restrictions, such as medicines, steroids, illegal pornography, firearms, weapons or illicit drugs? Yes No
2. More than 2250mL of alcohol or 50 cigarettes or 50g of tobacco products? Yes No
3. Goods obtained overseas or purchased duty and/or tax free in Australia with a combined total price of more than AUD$900, including gifts? Yes No
4. Goods/samples for business/commercial use? Yes No
5. AUD$10,000 or more in Australian or foreign currency equivalent? Yes No

   Note: If a customs or police officer asks, you must report travellers cheques, cheques, money orders or other bearer negotiable instruments of any amount.

6. Meat, poultry, fish, seafood, eggs, dairy, fruit, vegetables? Yes No
7. Grains, seeds, bulbs, straw, nuts, plants, parts of plants, traditional medicines or herbs, wooden articles? Yes No
8. Animals, parts of animals, animal products including equipment, pet food, eggs, biologicals, specimens, birds, fish, insects, shells, bee products? Yes No
9. Soil, items with soil attached or used in freshwater areas e.g. sports/recreational equipment, shoes? Yes No
10. Have you been in contact with farms, farm animals, wilderness areas or freshwater streams/lakes etc in the past 30 days? Yes No
11. Were you in Africa, South/Central America or the Caribbean in the last 6 days? Yes No

DECLARATION

The information I have given is true, correct and complete. I understand failure to answer any questions may have serious consequences.

YOUR SIGNATURE

Day Month Year

TURN OVER THE CARD

English

图 2-2-14　澳大利亚入境卡正面

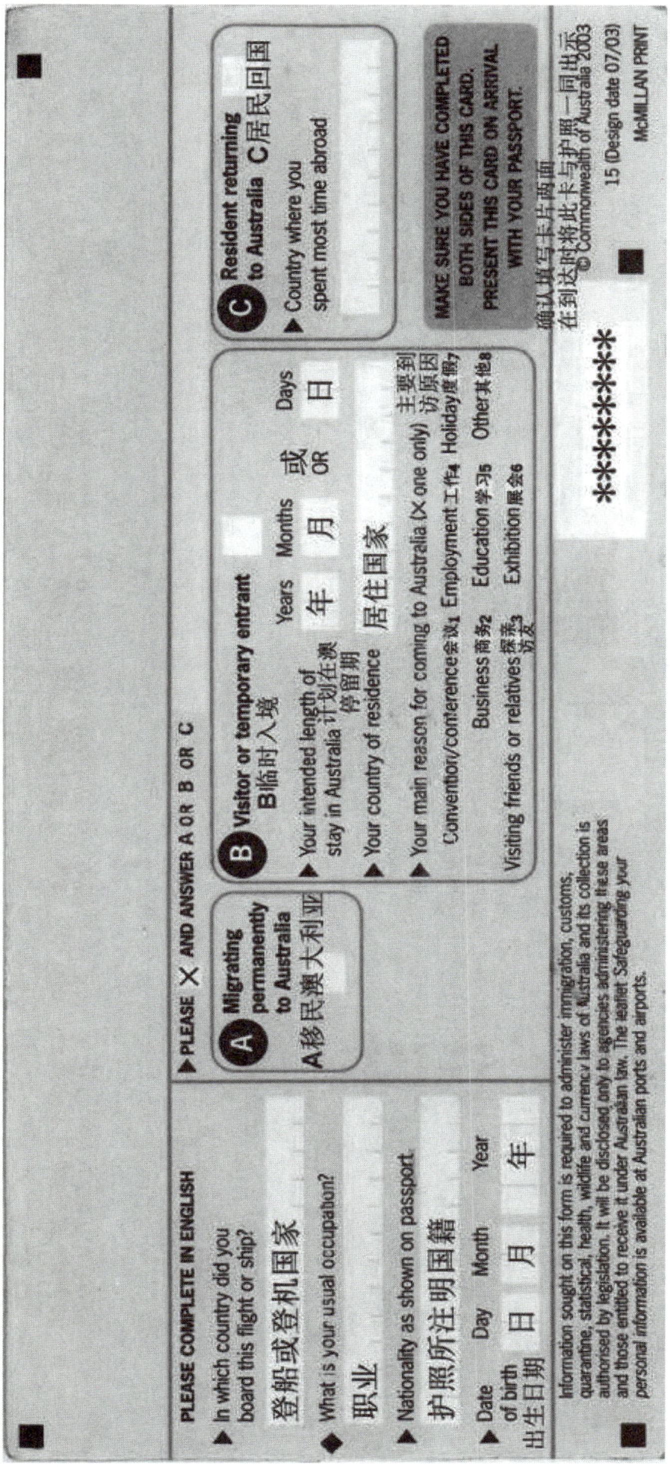
PLEASE COMPLETE IN ENGLISH

In which country did you board this flight or ship? 登船或登机国家

What is your usual occupation? 职业

Nationality as shown on passport 护照所注明国籍

Date of birth 出生日期 Day 日 Month 月 Year 年

PLEASE X AND ANSWER A OR B OR C

A Migrating permanently to Australia A移民澳大利亚

B Visitor or temporary entrant B临时入境

Your intended length of stay in Australia 计划在澳停留期 Years 年 Months 月 或 OR Days 日

Your country of residence 居住国家

Your main reason for coming to Australia (X one only) 主要到访原因

Convention/conference 会议1 Employment 工作4 Holiday 度假7

Business 商务2 Education 学习5 Other 其他8

Visiting friends or relatives 探亲访友3 Exhibition 展会6

C Resident returning to Australia C居民回国

Country where you spent most time abroad

MAKE SURE YOU HAVE COMPLETED BOTH SIDES OF THIS CARD. PRESENT THIS CARD ON ARRIVAL WITH YOUR PASSPORT.

确认填写卡片两面

在到达时将此卡与护照一同出示

Information sought on this form is required to administer immigration, customs, quarantine, statistical, health, wildlife and currency laws of Australia and its collection is authorised by legislation. It will be disclosed only to agencies administering these areas and those entitled to receive it under Australian law. The leaflet Safeguarding your personal information is available at Australian ports and airports.

****

© Commonwealth of Australia 2003

15 (Design date 07/03)

McMILLAN PRINT

图 2-2-15　澳大利亚入境卡反面

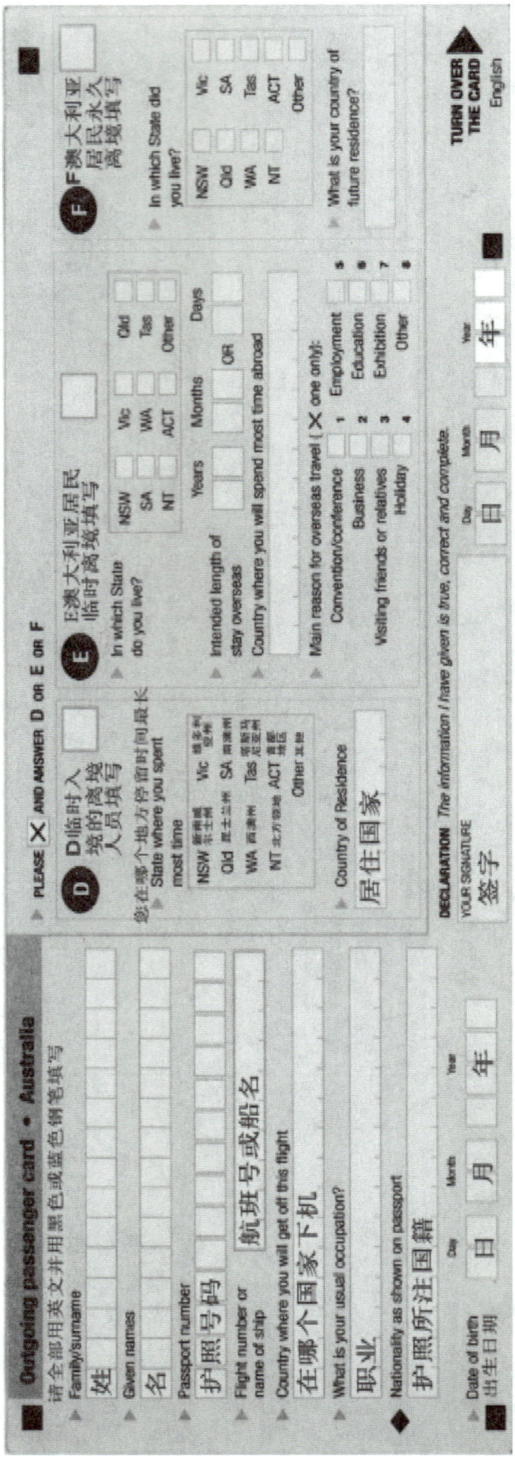

Outgoing passenger card • Australia

请全部用英文并用黑色或蓝色钢笔填写

Family/surname 姓

Given names 名

Passport number 护照号码

Flight number or name of ship 航班号或船名

Country where you will get off this flight 在哪个国家下机

What is your usual occupation? 职业

Nationality as shown on passport 护照所注国籍

Date of birth 出生日期 Day 日 Month 月 Year 年

PLEASE X AND ANSWER D OR E OR F

D 临时入境的离境人员填写

您在哪个地方停留时间最长 State where you spent most time

NSW Vic Qld SA WA Tas NT ACT Other

Country of Residence 居住国家

E 澳大利亚居民临时离境填写

In which State do you live? NSW Vic Qld SA WA Tas NT ACT Other

Intended length of stay overseas Years Months OR Days

Country where you will spend most time abroad

Main reason for overseas travel (X one only:

Convention/conference 1 Employment 5

Business 2 Education 6

Visiting friends or relatives 3 Exhibition 7

Holiday 4 Other 8

F 澳大利亚居民永久离境填写

In which State did you live? NSW Vic Qld SA WA Tas NT ACT Other

What is your country of future residence?

DECLARATION The information I have given is true, correct and complete.

YOUR SIGNATURE 签字 Day 日 Month 月 Year 年

TURN OVER THE CARD

English

图 2-2-16 澳大利亚出境卡

第八节 新西兰

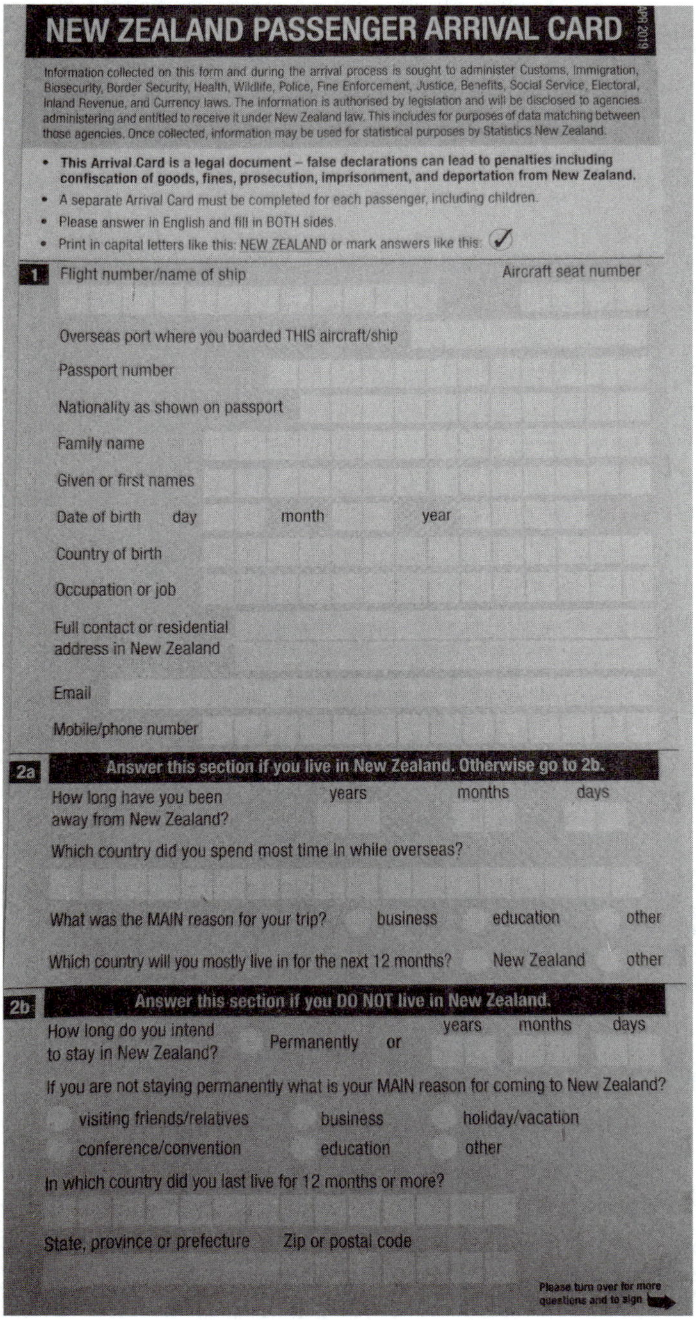

NEW ZEALAND PASSENGER ARRIVAL CARD

APR 2019

Information collected on this form and during the arrival process is sought to administer Customs, Immigration, Biosecurity, Border Security, Health, Wildlife, Police, Fine Enforcement, Justice, Benefits, Social Service, Electoral, Inland Revenue, and Currency laws. The information is authorised by legislation and will be disclosed to agencies administering and entitled to receive it under New Zealand law. This includes for purposes of data matching between those agencies. Once collected, information may be used for statistical purposes by Statistics New Zealand.

- **This Arrival Card is a legal document – false declarations can lead to penalties including confiscation of goods, fines, prosecution, imprisonment, and deportation from New Zealand.**
- A separate Arrival Card must be completed for each passenger, including children.
- Please answer in English and fill in BOTH sides.
- Print in capital letters like this: NEW ZEALAND or mark answers like this: ✓

1 Flight number/name of ship Aircraft seat number

Overseas port where you boarded THIS aircraft/ship

Passport number

Nationality as shown on passport

Family name

Given or first names

Date of birth day month year

Country of birth

Occupation or job

Full contact or residential address in New Zealand

Email

Mobile/phone number

2a Answer this section if you live in New Zealand. Otherwise go to 2b.

How long have you been away from New Zealand? years months days

Which country did you spend most time in while overseas?

What was the MAIN reason for your trip? business education other

Which country will you mostly live in for the next 12 months? New Zealand other

2b Answer this section if you DO NOT live in New Zealand.

How long do you intend to stay in New Zealand? Permanently or years months days

If you are not staying permanently what is your MAIN reason for coming to New Zealand?

visiting friends/relatives business holiday/vacation

conference/convention education other

In which country did you last live for 12 months or more?

State, province or prefecture Zip or postal code

Please turn over for more questions and to sign

图 2-2-17 新西兰入境卡正面

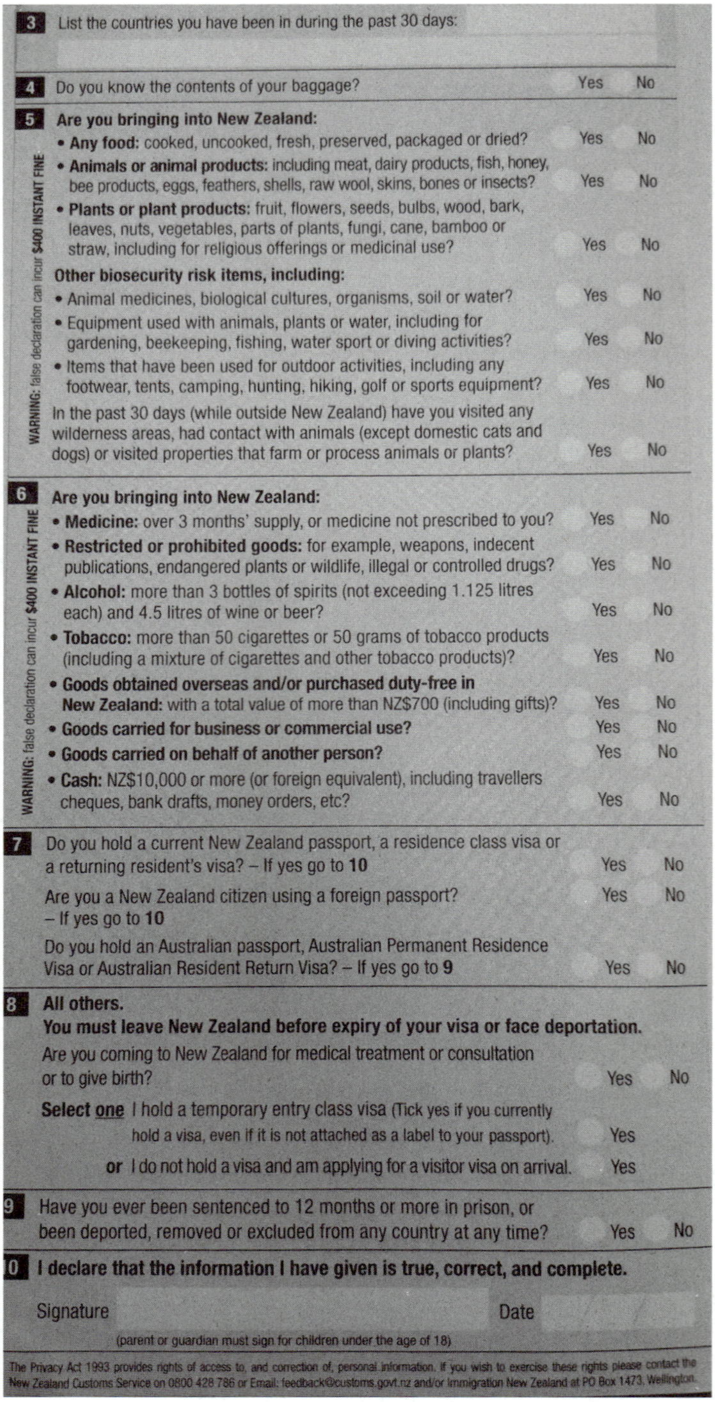

3 List the countries you have been in during the past 30 days:

4 Do you know the contents of your baggage? Yes No

5 **Are you bringing into New Zealand:**

- **Any food:** cooked, uncooked, fresh, preserved, packaged or dried? Yes No
- **Animals or animal products:** including meat, dairy products, fish, honey, bee products, eggs, feathers, shells, raw wool, skins, bones or insects? Yes No
- **Plants or plant products:** fruit, flowers, seeds, bulbs, wood, bark, leaves, nuts, vegetables, parts of plants, fungi, cane, bamboo or straw, including for religious offerings or medicinal use? Yes No

Other biosecurity risk items, including:

- Animal medicines, biological cultures, organisms, soil or water? Yes No
- Equipment used with animals, plants or water, including for gardening, beekeeping, fishing, water sport or diving activities? Yes No
- Items that have been used for outdoor activities, including any footwear, tents, camping, hunting, hiking, golf or sports equipment? Yes No

In the past 30 days (while outside New Zealand) have you visited any wilderness areas, had contact with animals (except domestic cats and dogs) or visited properties that farm or process animals or plants? Yes No

WARNING: false declaration can incur **$400 INSTANT FINE**

6 **Are you bringing into New Zealand:**

- **Medicine:** over 3 months' supply, or medicine not prescribed to you? Yes No
- **Restricted or prohibited goods:** for example, weapons, indecent publications, endangered plants or wildlife, illegal or controlled drugs? Yes No
- **Alcohol:** more than 3 bottles of spirits (not exceeding 1.125 litres each) and 4.5 litres of wine or beer? Yes No
- **Tobacco:** more than 50 cigarettes or 50 grams of tobacco products (including a mixture of cigarettes and other tobacco products)? Yes No
- **Goods obtained overseas and/or purchased duty-free in New Zealand:** with a total value of more than NZ$700 (including gifts)? Yes No
- **Goods carried for business or commercial use?** Yes No
- **Goods carried on behalf of another person?** Yes No
- **Cash:** NZ$10,000 or more (or foreign equivalent), including travellers cheques, bank drafts, money orders, etc? Yes No

WARNING: false declaration can incur **$400 INSTANT FINE**

7 Do you hold a current New Zealand passport, a residence class visa or a returning resident's visa? – If yes go to **10** Yes No

Are you a New Zealand citizen using a foreign passport? – If yes go to **10** Yes No

Do you hold an Australian passport, Australian Permanent Residence Visa or Australian Resident Return Visa? – If yes go to **9** Yes No

8 **All others.**

You must leave New Zealand before expiry of your visa or face deportation.

Are you coming to New Zealand for medical treatment or consultation or to give birth? Yes No

Select one I hold a temporary entry class visa (Tick yes if you currently hold a visa, even if it is not attached as a label to your passport). Yes

or I do not hold a visa and am applying for a visitor visa on arrival. Yes

9 Have you ever been sentenced to 12 months or more in prison, or been deported, removed or excluded from any country at any time? Yes No

10 **I declare that the information I have given is true, correct, and complete.**

Signature Date

(parent or guardian must sign for children under the age of 18)

The Privacy Act 1993 provides rights of access to, and correction of, personal information. If you wish to exercise these rights please contact the New Zealand Customs Service on 0800 428 786 or Email: feedback@customs.govt.nz and/or Immigration New Zealand at PO Box 1473, Wellington.

图 2-2-18　新西兰入境卡反面

思考与练习

Practice

一、简答题

1. C、I、Q 分别是哪三个国际行政职能部门，中文全称和英文全称分别是什么？三个部门的主要职责是什么？

What are the C, I, Q, and their obligations in English?

2. 边防检查的旅客证件分别有哪些？请举例说明。

What travelers' documents do the immigration and inspections check?

二、表格填写

1. 旅客张强（男）于 2021 年 5 月 25 日搭乘中国国际航空公司航班 CA106 由北京入境美国纽约，随身携带物品有：美金 20 000 元，在入境时需要对所带物品进行申报，请帮助其填写海关申报单。

Passenger Zhang Qiang takes flight CA106 from Beijing to New York in the USA on 25th May, 2021, he brings USD 20,000 which should be declared when entry, please fill out the Customs Declaration form for him.

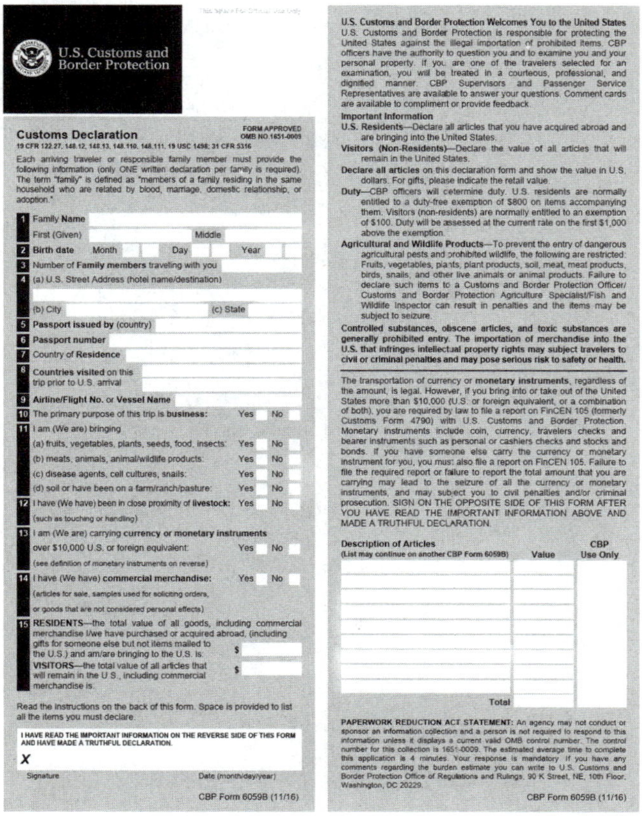

U.S. Customs and Border Protection

Customs Declaration

FORM APPROVED
OMB NO.1651-0009

19 CFR 122.27, 148.12, 148.13, 148.110, 148.111, 19 USC 1498; 31 CFR 5316

Each arriving traveler or responsible family member must provide the following information (only ONE written declaration per family is required). The term "family" is defined as "members of a family residing in the same household who are related by blood, marriage, domestic relationship, or adoption."

1 Family **Name**
First (Given) Middle
2 **Birth date** Month Day Year
3 Number of **Family members** traveling with you
4 (a) U.S. Street Address (hotel name/destination)
(b) City (c) State
5 **Passport issued by** (country)
6 **Passport number**
7 Country of **Residence**
8 **Countries visited** on this trip prior to U.S. arrival
9 **Airline/Flight No.** or **Vessel Name**
10 The primary purpose of this trip is **business:** Yes No
11 I am (We are) bringing
(a) fruits, vegetables, plants, seeds, food, insects: Yes No
(b) meats, animals, animal/wildlife products: Yes No
(c) disease agents, cell cultures, snails: Yes No
(d) soil or have been on a farm/ranch/pasture: Yes No
12 I have (We have) been in close proximity of **livestock:** Yes No
(such as touching or handling)
13 I am (We are) carrying **currency or monetary instruments** over $10,000 U.S. or foreign equivalent: Yes No
(see definition of monetary instruments on reverse)
14 I have (We have) **commercial merchandise:** Yes No
(articles for sale, samples used for soliciting orders, or goods that are not considered personal effects)
15 **RESIDENTS**—the total value of all goods, including commercial merchandise I/we have purchased or acquired abroad, (including gifts for someone else but not items mailed to the U.S.) and am/are bringing to the U.S. is: $
VISITORS—the total value of all articles that will remain in the U.S., including commercial merchandise is: $

Read the instructions on the back of this form. Space is provided to list all the items you must declare.

I HAVE READ THE IMPORTANT INFORMATION ON THE REVERSE SIDE OF THIS FORM AND HAVE MADE A TRUTHFUL DECLARATION.

X

Signature　　Date (month/day/year)

CBP Form 6059B (11/16)

U.S. Customs and Border Protection Welcomes You to the United States

U.S. Customs and Border Protection is responsible for protecting the United States against the illegal importation of prohibited items. CBP officers have the authority to question you and to examine you and your personal property. If you are one of the travelers selected for an examination, you will be treated in a courteous, professional, and dignified manner. CBP Supervisors and Passenger Service Representatives are available to answer your questions. Comment cards are available to compliment or provide feedback.

Important Information

U.S. Residents—Declare all articles that you have acquired abroad and are bringing into the United States.

Visitors (Non-Residents)—Declare the value of all articles that will remain in the United States.

Declare all articles on this declaration form and show the value in U.S. dollars. For gifts, please indicate the retail value.

Duty—CBP officers will determine duty. U.S. residents are normally entitled to a duty-free exemption of $800 on items accompanying them. Visitors (non-residents) are normally entitled to an exemption of $100. Duty will be assessed at the current rate on the first $1,000 above the exemption.

Agricultural and Wildlife Products—To prevent the entry of dangerous agricultural pests and prohibited wildlife, the following are restricted: Fruits, vegetables, plants, plant products, soil, meat, meat products, birds, snails, and other live animals or animal products. Failure to declare such items to a Customs and Border Protection Officer/Customs and Border Protection Agriculture Specialist/Fish and Wildlife Inspector can result in penalties and the items may be subject to seizure.

Controlled substances, obscene articles, and toxic substances are generally prohibited entry. The importation of merchandise into the U.S. that infringes intellectual property rights may subject travelers to civil or criminal penalties and may pose serious risk to safety or health.

The transportation of currency or **monetary instruments**, regardless of the amount, is legal. However, if you bring into or take out of the United States more than $10,000 (U.S. or foreign equivalent, or a combination of both), you are required by law to file a report on FinCEN 105 (formerly Customs Form 4790) with U.S. Customs and Border Protection. Monetary instruments include coin, currency, travelers checks and bearer instruments such as personal or cashiers checks and stocks and bonds. If you have someone else carry the currency or monetary instrument for you, you must also file a report on FinCEN 105. Failure to file the required report or failure to report the total amount that you are carrying may lead to the seizure of all the currency or monetary instruments, and may subject you to civil penalties and/or criminal prosecution. SIGN ON THE OPPOSITE SIDE OF THIS FORM AFTER YOU HAVE READ THE IMPORTANT INFORMATION ABOVE AND MADE A TRUTHFUL DECLARATION.

Description of Articles (List may continue on another CBP Form 6059B)	Value	CBP Use Only
Total		

PAPERWORK REDUCTION ACT STATEMENT: An agency may not conduct or sponsor an information collection and a person is not required to respond to this information unless it displays a current valid OMB control number. The control number for this collection is 1651-0009. The estimated average time to complete this application is 4 minutes. Your response is mandatory. If you have any comments regarding the burden estimate you can write to U.S. Customs and Border Protection Office of Regulations and Rulings, 90 K Street, NE, 10th Floor, Washington, DC 20229.

CBP Form 6059B (11/16)

2. 旅客 Eric Walton 于 2019 年 6 月 20 日搭乘 SQ293 由新加坡飞往印度尼西亚，在雅加达居住在世纪公园酒店 Century Park Hotel。请帮助其填写入境卡。

Passenger Eric Walton takes flight SQ293 from Singapore to Indonesia on 20th June, 2019. He lives in Century Park Hotel in Jakarta. Please fill in the entry form for him.

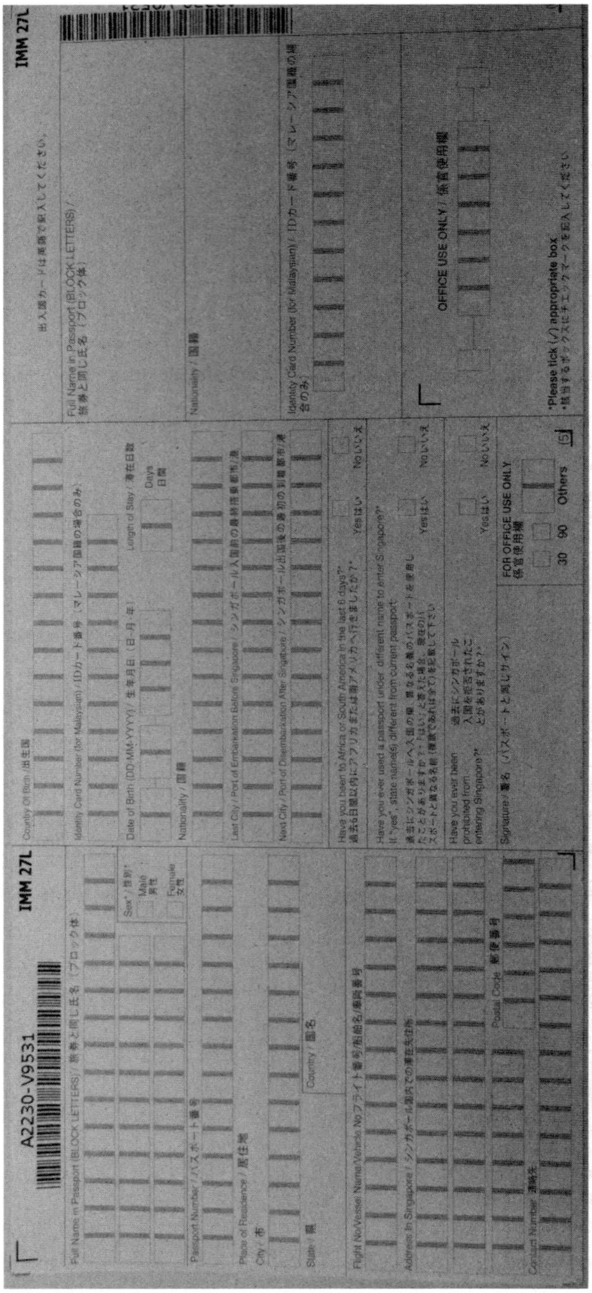
IMM 27L
A2230-V9531
Full Name in Passport (BLOCK LETTERS) / 旅券と同じ氏名（ブロック体）
Sex / 性別 Male 男性 Female 女性
Passport Number / パスポート番号
Place of Residence / 居住地
City / 市
State / 州
Country / 国名
Flight No/Vessel Name/Vehicle No
Address in Singapore
Postal Code 郵便番号
Contact Number 連絡先

Country of Birth / 出生国
Identity Card Number (for Malaysian)
Date of Birth (DD-MM-YYYY) / 生年月日（日-月-年）
Length of Stay / 滞在日数 Days 日数
Nationality / 国籍
Last City / Port of Embarkation Before Singapore
Next City / Port of Disembarkation After Singapore
Have you been to Africa or South America in the last 6 days? Yes はい No いいえ
Have you ever used a passport under different name to enter Singapore? If "yes", state name(s) different from current passport Yes はい No いいえ
Have you ever been prohibited from entering Singapore? Yes はい No いいえ
Signature / 署名
FOR OFFICE USE ONLY 30 90 Others

IMM 27L
Full Name in Passport (BLOCK LETTERS)
Nationality / 国籍
Identity Card Number (for Malaysian)
OFFICE USE ONLY
*Please tick (√) appropriate box

项目三　机上免税品销售

一、项目描述

随着国际航班的日益增多，机上免税品销售逐渐成为很多国际航班的重头戏。机上免税品种类繁多，包括香水、化妆品、保养品、配饰、腕表、皮具、数码、食品、玩具、名酒等。

各大航空公司会从品牌方获得一些专供在机上销售的套装和优惠价，成为“独家”商品，较专柜的价格更具吸引力。此外，航空公司也不断开发推出独具特色的产品，如飞机模型、地方特产、民族特色产品等，不断丰富旅行购物的选择空间。

通过本项目的学习让同学们了解国际航班上免税品销售的种类和规定，掌握机上免税品销售的服务流程；掌握主要国际流通货币的换算。

二、学习目标

（一）知识目标

1. 了解机上免税商品种类。
2. 了解免税品销售规定。
3. 了解外币和兑换。

（二）能力目标

1. 能够对免税品进行销售。
2. 能够对外币进行换算。

（三）素养目标

1. 学生具备更加专业、严谨的职业素养和态度，拓展专业知识范畴，树立为旅客提供高品质服务的信心。

2. 具有良好的职业道德与契约精神，良好的与人沟通能力和团队合作精神。

3. 具有爱国、敬业、诚信、友善的精神，服务乘客、服务社会的职业精神。

单元一 机上免税品销售服务

第一节 机上销售和免税品介绍

1. 机上销售的意义

（1）国际航班服务之一，为旅客提供高服务质量。

（2）为公司创造效益，增加个人收入，有助于个人的发展和技能提升。

2. 免税商品的介绍

免税品的定义：免税品是指经营单位按照海关核准的经营品种免税运进专供其免税店向规定的对象销售、供应的进口商品。

免税店经营的免税品品种，应由经营单位统一报经海关总署批准后，方可售卖。

免税品种类有：香烟、酒类、化妆品、香水、手表、首饰、礼品。

第二节 销售规定

1. 地面检查（Ground Check）

（1）负责销售的乘务长和乘务员登机后，检查免税车铅封是否完好，“核销单”上有海关印章、货物数量、铅封号及装配员签名。

The purser and cabin crew who are in charge of duty free check if all duty-free trolleys are locked when they get on board, they need to check the customs seal, quantity, seal number and signature by loader.

（2）核对免税车上铅封号与“核销单”上的铅封号一致。

Match the seal number on the duty-free trolley with the number on the form.

（3）如有异常，报告带班乘务长。

Report the chief purser if irregularities.

（4）保留铅封锁至清点正确无误后再扔掉。

Reserve the seal lock until inventoried.

2. 销售前清点（Inventory before sales）

（1）乘务长处领钥匙，两人清点。

Count the quantity of duty-free articles after getting the key from the purser.

（2）免税品有不符或破损，及时报告乘务长。

Report to purser if irregularities.

（3）保留铅封至清点无误后再扔掉。

Reserve the seal lock until inventoried.

（4）清点物品：销售明细单、销售记录表、刷卡机（刷卡单据）。

Inventory the articles: sales detail list, recording form, POS.

3. 销售时间（Sales time）

（1）销售前应广播通知旅客。

Make the duty-free sales cabin announcement before sales.

（2）一餐后开始进行免税品销售。

Start sales after the first meal service.

（3）国际航线的国内段不得进行免税品的销售。

The duty-free sales is not available on domestic stretch.

（4）遵守美国海关规定，在美国境内不得出售免税品。

The duty-free sales is not allowed in the border of the United States of America.

第三节　销售程序

销售程序及注意事项详见表 3-1-1。

表 3-1-1 销售程序及注意事项

Sales Procedure	
Duty-free articles located in galley (Night flight)	夜航飞行，为保障旅客休息，采用定点全员销售形式：免税品放置在不临近两舱的中/后厨房内，乘务员手持购物指南向旅客介绍，对于需要购买的旅客引导至厨房内购买，或由乘务员协助预订、拿取免税品
Start from first class/business class	免税品销售原则上从头等舱公务舱开始，免税品车不可进入两舱，由两舱乘务员根据旅客需求提供免税品
Charge in sales	免税品销售时，货款需当面向旅客清点。如零钱不足，征得旅客同意，找还等值的其他货币。如当时无法解决零钱问题，记下该旅客的座位号，尽快解决
Square accounts	账目清楚，单据由乘务员填写，乘务长核实并签字。 销售时，乘务员负责货品，乘务长负责货款，结账时由乘务长负责。 严格按比例提成
Notice	
Only duty-free articles on board	严禁销售机上免税品以外的物品
Notify passengers with the Customs regulations of the destination country (area)	掌握到达国家（地区）的海关规定，提前告知旅客，避免旅客购买超额免税品后要求退换
Monitor the duty-free articles during flight	销售过程中注意监控免税车，避免物品丢失。 销售过程中，各个厨房均应有乘务员监控
Meet the sleeping passengers' duty-free shopping demands	旅客在睡醒后如需购买免税品，乘务员应重新推出免税车，不能以免税品已结账为由拒绝旅客
Make the cabin announcement before suspending sales	停止出售免税品前，应广播通知旅客

续表

Refund & Exchange	
Not refundable articles	烟、酒、食品、化妆品等直接关系人体健康的商品，已经打开包装或使用过的不承诺退换货
Refund or exchange when quality problem	若乘客在本航班购物后发现有质量问题，经过乘务员确认后，可以办理退换货，并做好记录。 如质量无问题，不予退换
Refund or exchange demands on different flight	旅客在不同航班上购买的免税品拿到其他航班上要求退货时请婉言拒绝，并请该旅客与本公司联络退换货事宜

支付方式详见表 3-1-2。

表 3-1-2　支付方式

Available currency	US dollar, Euro, South-Korean Won, Japanese Yen, Australian dollar, Pound, Canada dollar, Hong Kong dollar,Chinese RMB, Singapore dollar
Currency exchange rate	Ask cabin attendants about the currency exchange rate between Chinese RMB and other major foreign currencies for detailed information
Credit card	MasterCard, JCB, American Express, Diners Club International, VISA

单元二　外币识别及计算

第一节　外币的识别与换算

一、现金

（1）只收汇率表中列明的币种（国际通用货币）。

（2）熟悉当日汇率、正确换算。

（3）太旧、残缺的钱不收。

（4）口齿清晰、唱钱。

（5）收整原则。

表 3-2-1　国际货币名称及代码缩写

货币名	国际代码和缩写符号	辅币进位
美元 US DOLLAR	USD US$	1 dollar=100 cents
欧元 EURO	EUR	1 EUR=100 cents
英镑 POUND	GBP £	1 pound=100 cents
加拿大元 CANADA DOLLAR	CAD CAN$	1 dollar=100 cents
澳大利亚元 AUSTRALIA DOLLAR	AUD A$	1 dollar=100 cents
韩元 KOREA WON	KRW KW	1 Won=100 cents
日元 JAPANESE YEN	JPY J ￥	1 yen=100 钱
新加坡元 SINGAPORE DOLLAR	SGD S$	1 dollar=100 cents
泰国铢 BAHT	THB	1 铢=100 satang
尼泊尔币 RUPEE	NPR	1 卢比=100 比萨
港币 HONGKONG DOLLAR	HKD HK$	1 dollar=100 cents
澳门币 PATACA	MOP	1 元=100 cents

二、汇率

货币外汇汇率，简称 FXRate，是英文“Foreign Exchange Rate”（外汇汇率）的缩写。是以本国货币来表示外国货币的价格，其高低最终由外汇市场决定。

假如：

- USD1.00＝RMB 6.5
- USD1.00＝JPY80.5
- USD1.00＝GBP0.5

请计算：

RMB1950.00＝USD

GBP950.00＝JPY

第二节　刷卡机及信用卡使用

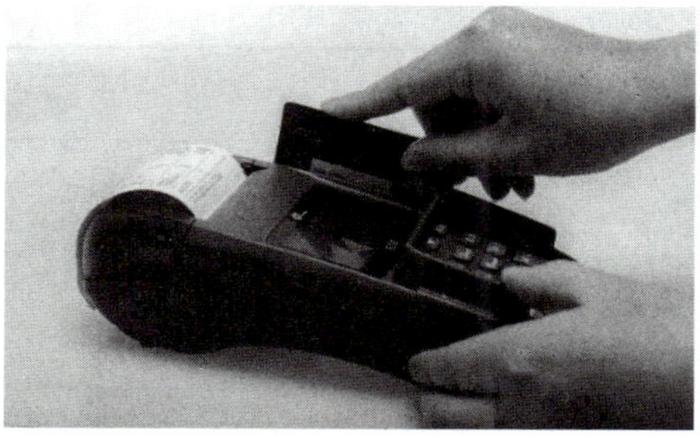

图 3-2-1　刷卡机

一、可接受信用卡类别

图 3-2-2　各大信用卡标志

目前大部分航空公司接受三种信用卡：JCB 日本信用卡；VISA 卡；万事达卡。

二、信用卡检查

信用卡检查内容详见表 3-2-2。

表 3-2-2　信用卡检查内容

Validity date	属可接受的信用卡范围，在有效期，当月到期的卡不接收
Unusable indication	卡上应没有 VALID ONLY IN XX、人民币结算、非外汇卡、只限 XX 地区使用等标识
Signature by card holder	背面有持卡人签名
Passport needed	要求旅客出示护照

三、刷卡机及信用卡使用注意事项

刷卡机及信用卡使用注意事项详见表 3-2-3。

表 3-2-3 刷卡机及信用卡注意事项

Using frequency limitation	每张信用卡只能刷一次
Monetary limitation	金额限制 USD15.00—USD499.00（以各航空公司标准为准）
Filling limitation	卡单上拓印若不清晰，不得描画；填写刷卡单出现错误时，应当着旅客面撕毁，重新使用新的刷卡单进行刷卡后填写

四、钱袋

钱袋注意事项详见表 3-2-4。

表 3-2-4 钱袋注意事项

Reserve cash	原则上应将备用金剩出，若无零钱，应注明钱袋内含备用金
Put-in items	钱袋内只装现金和卡单，不装销售单据
Sealing condition	三人在场，方可黏贴封钱袋
Storage	钱袋需在免税品车内

思考与练习

Practice

一、简答题 Short Answer Questions

1. 免税品的种类有哪些，举例说明。

Please list the duty free articles category.

2. 机上免税品销售可以接受哪些币种，举例说明。

Which currencies are acceptable in duty free sale?

3. 请列举信用卡检查事项。

Please list the credit card check matters.

4. 根据汇率计算。

如果 USD1.00=RMB 6.5　　USD1.00=JPY80.5　　USD1.00=GBP0.5

请计算：

RMB2080.00=USD_________

GBP260.00=JPY___________

二、计算题 Calculation

1. 某航班有一位客人购买了一瓶白兰地、一瓶威士忌、两条香烟、一个打火机。白兰地 USD27.00，威士忌 USD30.00，香烟 USD12.00，打火机 USD40.00。

如果汇率：USD1.00=HKD8.00

请问：应付多少港币？客人付 1 000 港币，应找回多少美元？

A passenger purchases one bottle of brandy, one bottle of whiskey, two cartons of cigarette, one fire lighter.

The price of the items: brandy USD27.00, whiskey USD30.00, cigarette USD12.00, fire lighter USD40.00

Exchange rate: USD1.00=HKD8.00

Question: How much to pay in HKD? How much to give change when he pays 1,000 HKD?

2. 某航班有一位旅客买了两条 555 牌香烟，一瓶威士忌。香烟 USD12.00，威士忌 USD141.00。

如果汇率：USD1.00=GBP0.70

请问：应付多少美元？应付多少英镑？

A passenger purchases two cartons of 555 cigarette, one bottle of whiskey.

The price of the items: cigarette USD12.00, whiskey USD141.00.

Exchange rate: USD1.00=GBP0.70

Question: How much to pay in USD and in GBP?

参考文献

[1] 陈艳秋，史亚杰. 民航持续安全的理论与实践[M]. 北京：中国民航出版社，2010.
[2] 黄速建，肖红军. 海航集团考察[M]. 北京：经济管理出版社，2015.
[3] 杨文锋. 民用航空质量管理理论与应用[M]. 成都：西南交通大学出版社，2015.
[4] 江群，王春. 民航基础知识应用[M]. 北京：国防工业出版社，2011.
[5] 万青. 航空运输地理[M]. 北京：中国民航出版社，2008.
[6] 杨桂芹，周为民. 民用航空航线·CIQ[M]. 北京：清华大学出版社，2013.
[7] 洪德慧，杨学峰. 航线地理[M]. 北京：科学出版社，2013.
[8] 廖正非，陈卓. 客舱服务[M]. 北京：电子工业出版社，2016.
[9] 杨长进，毕研博. 客舱服务[M]. 北京：航空工业出版社，2016.
[10] 方从法，罗茜. 民用航空概论[M]. 上海：上海交通大学出版社，2012.